D0114395

INTEGRITY

INTEGRITY

Ted W. Engstrom
with
Robert C. Larson

WORD BOOKS
PUBLISHER
WACO, TEXAS

A DIVISION OF
WORD, INCORPORATED

INTEGRITY

Copyright © 1987 by Ted W. Engstrom.

All rights reserved. No portion of this book may be
reproduced in any form without the written permission
of the publishers, with the exception of brief excerpts
quoted in magazine reviews.

Unless otherwise indicated all Scripture quotations are
taken from the New King James Version of the Bible,
copyright © 1979, 1980, 1982 by Thomas Nelson, Inc.
Used by permission.

Library of Congress Cataloging in Publication Data

Engstrom, Theodore Wilhelm, 1916–
   Integrity.

    1. Integrity.   2. Christian ethics.   3. United
States—Moral conditions.   I. Larson, Robert C.
II. Title.
BJ1533.158E54 1987   170'.973   87-25253
ISBN 0-8499-0634-2

  898 FG 9 8 7 6 5 4 3

Printed in the United States of America

To my dear friend

DR. RICHARD C. HALVERSON

Chaplain, U. S. Senate.
His lifetime of leadership
has modeled integrity.

Contents

∾ ──────────────── ∾

Foreword

Integrity is the word for our times! It may mean different things to different people, but it certainly means keeping our promises . . . doing what we said we would do . . . choosing to be accountable, and taking as our motto, *semper fidelis*—the promise to be *always faithful.*

If it is true that there are God-appointed eras for the emergence of pivotal ideas, then I'm confident there has never been a more critical time in our collective history for an insightful, challenging book on the subject of integrity. In this much needed volume, simply entitled, *Integrity,* my good friend and colleague in ministry, Dr. Ted Engstrom, has given us his best thinking yet, as he brings to our attention what he views as one of the profound issues of our time. What he has written about integrity needs to be read in the boardroom as well as the bedroom—in the family room and in the classroom. It is especially appropriate for the leaders of Christian ministries.

Sin is nothing new, of course. Telling lies and welshing on our promises are hardly unique to the latter part of the twentieth century. The impropriety of being unfaithful to one's spouse, or the tendency to wholesale tax cheating surely cannot be laid at the clay feet of an overgeneralized "social decay." However, through my travels, speaking and social research, I do get the overpowering sense that the *expression* of these evils appears to be increasing. Vast numbers of otherwise moral and well-meaning citizens seem to be denying the inherent value of their godly national roots, thus placing themselves and their families in moral jeopardy.

That's why I can say unequivocally that this book has come into our hands none too soon. Ted Engstrom, a Christian leader with deep concern for the vital issue of integrity, addresses the themes at hand with as poignant a message as I've ever seen him put on paper. However, far from a carping, critical spirit, his seasoned words of admonition, comfort, and counsel provide unbridled hope, along with a clearly marked path upon which he urges us all to travel.

I need this book. I'm confident you will echo that same sentiment as you allow its wisdom to flow through you to become part of your life. *Integrity* is a Godsend for troubled times.

DR. JAMES C. DOBSON

1

Semper Infidelis

1

Semper Infidelis

*When we can no longer depend on one another
to do what we said we would do, the future
becomes an undefined nightmare.*

> "When I did well, I heard it never;
> when I did ill, I heard it ever."
> *Old English Rhyme*

Semper Fidelis," always faithful—the official, etched-in-stone motto of the U.S. Marine Corps. But in the light of the sex-for-spying scandal in Moscow, the leathernecks are having to answer to "Semper INfidelis." For 200 years, and from the halls of Montezuma to the shores of Tripoli, the Marines have stood for loyalty, discipline, and faithfulness. We still hear it: "The Marines are looking for a few good men." Now, it seems, they're looking for more than just a few!

In early 1987 two Marine guards at the U.S. embassy in Moscow allegedly escorted Soviet agents into the most sensitive chambers of the consulate—including the "secure" communications center. The damage? Incalculable. Entire lists of secret agents, threatened. Transmission codes, compromised. Plans, immobilized.

And what force overpowered the men who had supposedly received the finest military training in the free world? Was it firearms? Torture? Nuclear blackmail? No, it was *sex*. Lust of the flesh held sway over the strength of armor.

But surely this incident was merely some bizarre exception. Who wants to believe our armed forces could be neutralized by the arms of women? I, for one, still have a great deal of confidence in our young soldiers. Maybe that's because I once wore the Army green as a young man myself. What concerns me most is not that something like this can happen in the U.S. Marines, but that it seems to be happening all over the world in so many other institutions. If a small, highly trained group of elite soldiers cannot take the hill, what of the civilians who follow behind?

What about our lawmakers? Do they obey their own laws? Have our preachers heard their own sermons on repentance? Is the business world sold on ethics? Are "lovers" truly loving one another? Are parents producing character in their children or just raising characters?

This morning, I threw down my copy of the *Los Angeles Times* in disgust. It was more of the same . . . filled with further explicit allegations of the sexual misconduct of a prominent TV evangelist, along with new stories about his wife's spending habits that are beginning to make Imelda Marcos seem conservative. As a fellow Christian, I believe in grace and forgiveness. But what makes this TV evangelist's sexual impropriety particularly damaging is that his tryst took place *seven years ago*. Allegedly, too, it involved drugged wine and unnatural acts against the woman's will. Not only that, he arranged payment of more than $265,000 in hush money. And he "confessed" only after the incident received national attention.

Like loose threads on a sweater, one revelation led to another. Next he announced the transfer of his entire nationwide broadcast organization to a rival preacher. Later he claimed that same preacher had seized control through a hostile takeover.

Several other well-known television ministers exchanged heated charges and countercharges with this "gospelebrity." Did he and his wife pocket undisclosed millions in bonuses and cash while claiming only a modest salary? Were there other sexual encounters? Are there any political figures involved?

The stakes behind this one prodigal personality are enormous: Thirteen million viewers, $172 million in assets, a 2,300-acre religious theme park (second only to Disneyland and Disney World in attendance). For lack of integrity, this evangelist lost it all.

Unfortunately, there are other prominent preachers calling the integrity of God's servants into question. Another evangelist retired to his prayer tower until supporters could raise eight million dollars to bail him out of acute financial difficulties relating to his medical school. If he didn't get the money, God was going to "call him home." Fortunately, the dollars arrived and he survived. Unfortunately, Christian integrity had once again been rushed into intensive care.

Semper Fidelis?

It's little wonder that in early 1987, pollster George Gallup, Jr., told a meeting of Christian fund-raisers that 42 percent of Americans doubted the honesty of some, if not most, appeals for religious donations.[1]

How well do some of these preachers tread water? Jesus warns us "whoever causes one of these little ones who believe in Me to sin, it would be better for him if a millstone were hung around his neck, and he were drowned in the depth of the sea" (Matt. 18:6). The masonry yard must be doing a land-office business in millstones these days.

What used to be looked upon as merely a desirable "Boy Scout" trait, integrity, is now proving itself to be the heart and soul of the whole person.

Oh, how the mighty are fallen! Major Wall Street financiers led off to jail in three-piece suits and handcuffs. These highrollers thought they could rewrite the commandment against stealing. A front-running presidential candidate forced to resign from the race. He mistakenly thought he had "executive privilege" when it came to the adultery command. Two of America's more promising athletes killed by cocaine (in separate incidents). They thought they were mightier, stronger, and more potent than natural laws of survival.

CHALLENGER

Not only can the lack of integrity kill the individual involved, it can also cut down whole groups of innocent people as well.

It was a chilly Tuesday morning, 28 January 1986, when Christa McAuliffe climbed aboard the Challenger space shuttle for her historic mission as the first citizen in space. She was a teacher. I only pray that we learned something about the consequences of getting an "F" in integrity. The weather was cold, but unbeknown to the rest of the nation a group of engineers was fighting back the hot sweat of worried anticipation. Would the booster seals hold in this kind of weather? Was it safe to launch? Knowledgeable engineers and designers said, "No." Influential executives and planners said, "Yes."

Power overruled reason. Integrity was the victim. After seventy seconds of flight, a faulty booster rocket ignited millions of gallons of rocket fuel into a blinding explosion. Debris rained on the Florida waters for a solid hour. At first we believed that Christa and the other six crew members perished instantly at the moment of explosion. Upon examination of the cabin remains, we have since learned they may have endured almost three and a half minutes of terrifying freefall before smashing into the Atlantic Ocean at 200 miles per hour. I only wish these words about the urgent need for integrity could carry that same force of impact.

ROAD TO RUIN

But only seven people died in this infraction of character. The space shuttle's destruction was dramatic. It was immortalized before the whole world on television. Much quieter is the steady slaughter of *tens of thousands* on the nation's highways. In the months since the Challenger accident extinguished seven heroes, the automobile has done the same for approximately 30,000 potential parents of heroes.

I'm confident that virtually every loss on the road can be traced to some form of loss in integrity. It's an established fact that at least one half of this nation's automobile accidents are caused by alcohol or substance abuse. The other half are always the fault of *someone's* less-than-wholehearted attention to detail, maintenance, or skill. Yes, I too have had my share of fright behind the wheel. And I know it's often the fault of the other guy, or the equipment. But that's my point. If you trace back any cause far enough, you'll find someone who forgot that these glass and steel "things" actually carry flesh-and-blood people. Perhaps I belabor the point. But maybe I can make you squirm enough to want to buckle up. That, too, involves integrity.

ACQUIRED INTEGRITY DEFICIENCY SYNDROME

Semper infidelis? Where else could this term have greater meaning than in family, marriage, and sex? Fidelity and integrity have always been an important part of family relationships. Now they, too, are becoming matters of life and death.

Acquired Immune Deficiency Syndrome, AIDS, has infected our headlines for the past several years. Now it's front page news almost every day. The implications are almost unfathomable—an incurable disease transmitted by the most difficult of human activities to discuss (much less control)—illicit sex. (I realize that contaminated needles among drug users are the second most common form of spreading AIDS. But as a man of the Word, I also realize that the sensual passion to rape one's own veins with a long phallic symbol for the purpose of arousing an orgasmic sensation by injecting narcotics is essentially the same lust of the flesh as illicit sex.)

"The life of the flesh is in the blood," we learn from Leviticus 17:11. And now, even more than ever before, we know it's true. Because with AIDS, the "death" of the flesh is in the blood.

If one were "always faithful," would it be possible to get AIDS? Sadly, yes. The infection is too far out of control. The world is simply too far from God. Through transfusions, pregnancy, nursing mothers, accidental exposure from wound to wound, and other methods, the iniquities of the "fathers" of AIDS can be visited upon another generation.

But not just "unto the third and fourth generation" as sins of old. This contagion is too lethal for that brief a lifespan. In a matter of months, AIDS can reduce a 180-pound athlete to an 80-pound spectator. In a few more weeks—to an obituary notice.

This lapse in integrity will fill whole columns of obituaries. The U.S. Surgeon General has estimated that approximately 179,000 Americans will die from AIDS by 1991.

If you printed two names per line, that many fatalities would require 83 pages of the *Los Angeles Times* listing from top to bottom, six columns across, no pictures, no ads.

And that total of 179,000 deaths by 1991 assumes most of those people who successfully produced AIDS antibodies in their blood would *not* die. The 1987 conference on AIDS in Washington, D.C., introduced evidence that most people who successfully produce antibodies in their blood *will* eventually contract the disease and die prematurely.

Frantic search is under way for better treatments and perhaps a cure. In the meantime, they tell us, the best we can do for ourselves is practice so-called "safe sex," avoid blood-to-blood contact, and practice monogamy.

Indeed monogamy needs practice. Far too many people are out of the habit or never knew how. What are the benefits of remaining "always faithful" to your mate? They used to be little more than convenience, comfort, and consideration. Today those benefits include existence itself.

THE LARGER ISSUE

It would be easy to fill this space with many other examples of infirm integrity. Other stories will surface in subsequent chapters. The chronology of human failures is endless. But the real question is not, "Who's involved in the latest failure?" It doesn't take much guts to hold up the faults of someone else to hide one's own shortcomings.

The larger issue is, what can you and I do *personally* to avoid our own failures and preserve our ability to serve? When Christ said, "Broad is the way that leads to destruction," He was not calling His disciples to jump on a spiritual bandwagon. He was warning and instructing them in a way of life.

What is *integrity?*

Let's keep it simple. I could give you a long, complicated dictionary answer about how *integrity* means "whole," "sound," and "unimpaired." But that's so much academia. What I'd rather do here is try to breathe some life into these empty syllables. Interact with me as we dress "integrity" up in work clothes and send it out to earn its keep in our everyday world.

PROMISE

Simply put, *Integrity* is doing what you said you would do. "One of the most fundamental acts of a society is promise-keeping," says Dr. Lewis Smedes, Professor of Theology and Christian Ethics at Fuller Theological Seminary in California. Here is the bedrock of social relationships. When we can no longer depend on one another to do what we said we would do, the future becomes an undefined nightmare.

Society makes promises to us. Governments make promises to us. Our friends make promises. The Church makes promises. All of these relate to the future. Each one says, "When the time comes, you can count on my coming through."

How different it sounds when, instead of talking about reviewing plans and objectives, we picture ourselves as reviewing the *promises* we have made and making new ones—at home and on the job.

To make a promise is a holy thing. In this book, with its simple title, *Integrity*—and as a fellow passenger on the same plane—I am committing a part of my life to you. I am announcing that you have an interest in my future. I am stating that you can expect your life to proceed as you would hope because of my willingness to fit into your needs and desires.

Thus *integrity*. Keeping promises. Doing what you said you would do.

SIXTEEN REFERENCES

Ironically, out of sixteen references in the Bible, the first time the word *integrity* occurs it is attributed to a pagan king as protection—against *God's* servant! Genesis 20 tells us that Abraham and Sarah both lied to Abimelech, king of Gerar, about Sarah's identity as a married woman. Therefore Abimelech "sent and took her" (v. 2). When God threatened to kill Abimelech if he committed adultery, Abimelech replied, "Lord, will you slay a righteous nation also? Did he not say to me, 'She is my sister'? And she even herself said, 'He is my brother.' In the *integrity* of my heart and innocence of my hands I have done this" (Gen. 20:5, emphasis mine).

God spared Abimelech's life and illustrated three important principles. 1) Integrity can be a life-and-death issue; 2) unbelievers can and do exhibit great integrity; and 3) need it be said even God's servants have feet of clay and often *do* fall painfully short of the ideal?

(If you want to pursue other references, check out these verses that deal with "integrity": Genesis 20:6; 1 Kings 9:4; Job 2:3, 9, 27:5; 31:6; Psalms 7:8; 25:21; 26:1, 11; 41:12; 78:72; Proverbs 11:3; 19:1; 20:7.)

HIDDEN REFERENCES

There's an interesting story about integrity hidden in the meaning of its Hebrew spelling.[2]

In the original Hebrew, *thom* signifies "whole" and "complete," thus it is translated as "integrity." But in the plural, *thummim* refers to part of the ceremonial accouterments worn by the High Priest, and him alone. Two special objects are mentioned in conjunction with the priest's decorative breastplate, the Urim and Thummim. "They shall be over Aaron's heart when he goes in before the Lord" (Exod. 28:30). Their exact function is a mystery. But we do know they were important objects because scripture tells us there were times when a high-level decision could not be made "until a priest could consult with the Urim and Thummim" (Ezra 2:63; Neh. 7:65).

Scholars are divided about their exact composition. Some think they were stone objects, others suggest they were another name for the twelve gemstones representing the twelve tribes of Israel. Another feels they were some kind of gold plate. But authorities all agree these items were important.

What does *thummim* have to do with integrity? As the plural of *thom*, this object suggests the perfections or *integrities* required to stand before God and discern His will. No High Priest could enter the Holy of Holies without his heart being covered by "perfections" (integrity). God wanted His priests to understand integrity. He also wants every Christian to be protected with the "breastplate of righteousness" and a spiritual *thummim* as well (Eph. 6:14).

INTEGRITY IN ACTION

Ideas in theory and ideas in action are seldom the same. But when one follows the other, there is the opportunity for change and growth. I appreciate the following story told by my friend and colleague, Robert Schuller.

KEEP ON SHINING

A judge was campaigning for reelection. He had a reputation for integrity. He was a distinguished and honorable gentleman of no small charity. His opponent was conducting a vicious, mud-smearing, unfair campaign against him.

Somebody approached the judge and asked, "Do you know what your opponent is saying about you? Do you know he is criticizing you? How are you going to handle it? What are you going to do about it?" The judge looked at his counselors and his campaign committee and calmly replied, "Well, when I was a boy I had a dog. And every time the moon was full, that hound dog would howl and bark at the bright face of the moon. We never did sleep very well those nights. He would bark and howl at the moon all night." With that, the judge concluded his remarks.

"That's beside the point," his campaign manager impatiently said. "You've told us a nice story about your dog, but what are you going to do about your critic?"

The judge explained, "I just answered you! When the dog barked at the moon, the moon kept right on shining! I don't intend to do anything but keep right on shining. And I'll ignore the criticism, as the moon ignored the dog. I'll just keep right on shining! Quietly, calmly, beautifully!"[3]

How about you? Just when this darkened world needs brightness the most, many of those around us have chosen to cloak themselves in shadows. You and I can choose otherwise. Obviously we won't attempt to believe we'll live out the rest of our lives in a state of perfection. But we *can* choose to be "semper fidelis" *this day.* Many successful rehabilitation programs teach people to make long-lasting changes by focusing on simple improvements "one day at a time." It might be well to remember that where a lifetime commitment seems overwhelming, "one day" can be manageable. And if you and I can demonstrate integrity in our lives *today*, it will be easier to do so again *tomorrow*, and the next day. But for now, one day is enough.

For today alone, I invite you to join me in an . . .

INTEGRITY ACTION PLAN #1

1. Not focusing on the evil around, but concentrating on the good within.
2. Giving your word and keeping it.
3. Clothing your body and your mind with excellence.
4. Promising to keep on shining.

Such a mutually agreed upon plan could solve the problem of "semper infidelis" overnight *if* this vale of tears in which we live wasn't so fettered by the chains of habit. To change *ourselves* and to appreciate the pulls on those who surround us, we need to understand some of the history behind these issues—our topic in Chapter 2.

2

One Nation under Greed?

*It seems ironic that as I write this chapter we are
now observing the fifteenth anniversary of a
watershed event in American ethics.*

> "For thirty pieces of silver, Judas
> sold himself, not Christ."
> *Hester H. Cholmondoly*

We Americans pledge allegiance to "one nation under God" and then often conduct our lives as if we believed in "one nation under greed." The currency in our pockets says, "In God We Trust," but which god? New cars, vacation homes, investments, prestige, and notoriety all develop heartbeats of their own, and rise up to demand our worship.

Chapter 1 showed us a parade of moral misfits answering to another god. But the overriding questions remain. *How* did our nation get this way? And what can we do to affect a *change?*

OPENING THE FLOODGATE

It seems ironic that as I write this chapter we are now observing the fifteenth anniversary of a watershed event in American ethics. It was early Saturday morning on 17 June 1972. A guard named Frank Wills noticed the catch on a door leading from his building into its garage had been taped so it would not lock. Thinking someone in the building had put it there, he tore off the tape. On his next rounds, Wills found the catch had been retaped. This time he called the police. The officers went to the eighth floor and started down. On the sixth floor, they surprised five men rifling files. Although they were dressed in suits and ties, they wore surgical gloves and carried walkie-talkies.

The newspapers didn't make much of the incident. It just didn't have the feel of a front-page news story. At least not yet.

The following Monday, President Nixon's press secretary Ronald Ziegler called it "a third-rate burglary," but with that small start began the biggest political scandal in American history.

In the ensuing years, the fallout from the Watergate incident would cause the first resignation of a president, the coincidental first resignation of a vice president, the trials and jailing of many top administration officials including the attorney general, the White House chief of staff, the head of the president's domestic counsel and his White House lawyer.

The White House attempted to hide its role in the affair and payoffs were made to the burglars.

In a conversation with his chief of staff, H. R. Haldeman, six days after the burglary, President Nixon agreed to a plan whereby the CIA, on a pretext that its operations might be compromised, would tell the FBI not to investigate Watergate further.

John Dean, the White House counsel who was involved in the planning of the political espionage effort, tried to tell Nixon how deeply mired the White House had become. When it became apparent prosecutors were closing in, Dean told them the whole story.

The House Judiciary Committee held hearings to

decide whether to recommend that Nixon be impeached, and voted yes on three of five charges. Then came the final blow: among the tape recordings Nixon had to release was the Haldeman conversation of 23 June 1972—dubbed the "smoking gun."

Two years later, on 8 August 1974, Nixon told the nation he had lost his political base. He resigned as of noon the next day.

TURNING POINT?

Many observers feel this event served as a critical turning point in America's moral conscience. Soon after the fall of Nixon a groundswell of sentiment spawned new interest in campaign reform and political honesty.

But how long did it last?

A recent poll by *U.S. News* and Cable News Network showed that more than half of the 1,006 adults surveyed think people are less honest today than they were ten years ago. Seven out of ten say they are dissatisfied with current standards of honesty—the largest proportion since 1973, at the height of the Watergate scandal.[1]

And those polled seem to be particularly suspicious of public figures. Three out of four say they rarely or never lie to family members, and substantial majorities of married respondents think their spouses are almost always honest with them. But only 30 percent feel that congressional leaders always or almost always tell the truth; only 38 percent believe the President "tells it like it is."

This reminds me of the old backwoods story. Seems a farmer needed an extra hand for a moment. "Will you hold my horse?" he said to a well-dressed stranger.

"Sir," said the stranger, "I'll have you know that I'm a member of the U.S. Congress."

"Oh, that's all right," said the farmer. "I'll trust you anyway."

Despite their dim view of what's going on in the outside world, those surveyed in this same poll indicated they personally still highly prized integrity. Overwhelmingly, they ranked it as the most important characteristic in a friend—well ahead of intelligence or even common interests. Those same respondents were firm in their convictions that others, up to and including public officials, should be held to high standards of honesty and integrity. Seven out of ten said the President of the United States should *never* lie to the American public.

Yet as I wrote this chapter, the news was filled with new revelations of President Reagan's alleged mishandling of the Iran-Contra arms and hostage affair. Senior staff members, cabinet members, military leaders, secretaries, and numerous others paraded before the congressional committee on television interpreting and inventing the truth. Many sought to uncover yet another "smoking gun" in the hand of the President. A political cartoon showed President Reagan assuring us there was no smoking gun in this incident. Slumped across his desk was a face-down body with a knife in its back.

LEADERS TURNED LOSERS

Americans have been given ample cause for alarm. In a recent cover story on "Ethics," *Time* magazine ran the following revelation. "More than 100 members of the Reagan Administration have had ethical or legal charges leveled against them. That number is without precedent."[2]

Not counting those embroiled in the "Iran-amuk" crisis, the infamous include: a Secretary of Labor who was indicted for his company's involvement in defrauding the

New York City Transit Authority of $7.4 million; a Chief of the FAA who resigned when grand juries probed his earlier business dealings; a Food and Drug Administration Commissioner who resigned while under investigation for over- lapping reimbursements for travel; a National Security Adviser who resigned amid controversy over a $1,000 "honorarium"; an EPA Assistant Administrator who was convicted of perjury concerning preferential treatment given to a former employer, to cite but a few.

The article went on to state, "While the Reagan Administration's missteps may not have been as flagrant as the Teapot Dome scandal or as pernicious as Watergate, they seem more general, more pervasive and somehow more ingrained than those of any previous Administration. During other presidencies, scandals such as Watergate seemed to multiply from a single cancer; the Reagan Administration, however, appears to have suffered a breakdown of the immune system, opening the way to all kinds of ethical and moral infections."[3]

PERSONAL REFLECTION

The natural reaction is to look at these evildoers, hike up our skirts, and turn smugly away in righteous indignation. But before you and I assume the role of prosecutor, judge, and executioner, let's take a look at ourselves.

I'll start with me. (To keep you reading, I'll say now that I'm saving my personal edition of a "sinner's scrapbook" for Chapter 6.) But one short incident will serve to remind me of my need to examine my own motives and actions.

It was back in 1944 while I was serving both in the U.S. Army and as editor of *Christian Digest* magazine for Pat and Bernie Zondervan. We were on a troop train.

Before my conversion I enjoyed an occasional poker game, but for reasons of conscience gave it up soon afterward. However, this trip was long and the train was slow, so when a couple of the fellows invited me to join them for a few hands, I hesitated only a moment before saying, "Deal me in."

I knew I shouldn't be playing. My conscience was smarting the whole time. But then nobody was going to recognize me so why not keep playing? During the game, I noticed a young man who stood to watch me play for a while, then moved on. After the game was over, this same young soldier approached again.

"Are you Ted Engstrom?" he asked.

"Yes," I replied.

"Are you the Ted Engstrom who writes that column in the *Christian Digest?*"

"Yes, I am. Why? Have we met?"

"No, we haven't met, but I read that column all the time."

About now I could feel the flush of embarrassment and consternation rising with more intensity than the thrill of four aces.

"Well, I want you to know that I've lost all respect for you." Then he turned and walked away from me (and perhaps the Lord). I never saw that soldier again.

No big deal? Hardly. It started as an innocent little game to kill time, but I soon discovered the stakes were much higher. Now it was no game and the issue had grown as large as my entire ministry and a brother's spiritual well-being. I've never forgotten the pain and sadness of that moment.

It's sobering to think how quickly the smallest personal decision can escalate into a large group concern. I'm sure the people whose pictures appeared in that *Time* article could all tell similar stories about the innocent beginnings of their ordeal.

It's obvious the Watergate debacle didn't bring lasting reform to the secular world, so it should come as little surprise that previous problems in the pulpit didn't prevent our current religious difficulties.

SEDUCTION AND ADULTERY

One of the early celebrity preacher scandals involved sex and a clergyman who—like today's group of miscreants—also enjoyed "the good life." Before and after the Civil War, the Rev. Henry Ward Beecher was the most famous preacher in the land. His oratory drew crowds of thousands to his church in Brooklyn each week. Some called him "the greatest preacher since Saint Paul." He reportedly earned the princely (and unheard-of) sum of $40,000 per year. Delighting in his treasures, Beecher enjoyed carrying with him uncut gems and openly endorsed commercial products ranging from soap to watches. Then in 1874 Beecher's friend and protegé, Theodore Tilton, accused the beloved preacher of seducing his wife. The trial was such an attraction that admission tickets were sold to the public. And the outcome? The jury failed to reach a verdict but Beecher's influence and popularity continued undiminished for another thirteen years until his death.

FALLEN "QUEEN OF HEAVEN"

Another notorious case of an imperfect pastor in America occurred some fifty years later. She was flamboyant and attractive—a seemingly necessary mix for the flapper age of the Roaring Twenties. Aimee Semple

McPherson wore flowing white gowns as she held court in her $1.5 million church in Los Angeles where she was surrounded by choirs, bell-ringers, and an eighty-piece xylophone band. One afternoon in May of 1926, at the peak of her career, McPherson went for a swim in the Pacific and disappeared.

Thirty-six days later she emerged in a Mexican border town, claiming to have wandered through the desert after escaping from kidnapers. Police, noting that the ordeal had left her shoes unscuffed, turned up evidence that the preacher had in fact spent most of the time in a Carmel, California, cottage with a former employee, himself married. McPherson was charged with "conspiracy to commit acts injurious to public morals."

Though the case was eventually dropped and the "Queen of Heaven's" flock remained loyal, McPherson died at the age of fifty-three of an "accidental overdose" of barbiturates.

You and I would like to think experiences such as these teach us something. I'm sure they do. But not always as much as we would like.

DONOR DOLLARS

In the late 1970s I had the privilege and pain of reviewing our country's charitable giving practices. This experience led to the formation of a national council. The country had undergone a prominent scandal some years earlier involving the Pallottine Fathers. In 1975, two reporters for the *Baltimore Sun* discovered that the Pallottine order, mailing as many as a hundred million letters a year in charity appeals, was funneling large sums into a variety of other operations—monetary and political. They collected millions of dollars that donors thought were going to the poor. This deception—along with several other public disclosures—spurred many religious organizations into a closer examination of their financial dealings.

Over 150,000 inquiries a year poured into the Better Business Bureau concerning the "honesty" of charitable organizations.

In December 1977, representatives of thirty-two evangelical Christian groups met in Chicago to decide on their response to mounting pressure for reform. Over the next few months, a steering committee developed standards which would be applicable to evangelical groups and sought to communicate with others who were not at the original sessions. In March 1979, the Evangelical Council for Financial Accountability (ECFA) was formed, representing more than 1,100 evangelical organizations with a total 1975 income of $1 billion from 25 to 30 million donors. It was my privilege to serve as chairman of the board at the ECFA for its first three years.

Today, this organization accounts for approximately $1.5 billion in donations. Unfortunately the American Association of Fund-Raising Council estimates that religious causes collect around $37 billion. Who oversees the remaining $35.5 billion?[4]

I'll have more to say about ECFA and its standards for fair fund-raising in Chapter 7.

ONE EMPIRE UNDER GREED

America's experience with greed and integrity breakdown is by no means the first. The events which led to the collapse of the Roman Empire are startlingly similar to the events occurring in our nation today.

The following seven-step sequence was recently distributed as a warning to America by the Arthur S. DeMoss Foundation. I find its conclusions revealing and sobering:

Historical Sequence

1. Strong Families: Rome was founded on high moral standards. Each father was respected as the head of the family. In the early republic, the father had legal authority to discipline rebellious members of his family.
2. Home Education: The education of the children was the responsibility of the parents. This further strengthened the children's honor and respect for their parents and also deepened the communication and understanding between parents and children.
3. Prosperity: Strong Roman families produced a strong nation. The Roman armies were victorious in war. The wealth of conquered nations increased Roman prosperity and prestige.
4. National Achievements: Great building programs began in Rome. A vast network of roads united the empire. Magnificent palaces, public buildings, and coliseums were constructed.
5. Infiltration of "The Lie": ("The Lie" was first given to Eve in the garden of Eden: ". . . ye shall be as gods, knowing—and deciding for yourselves—good and evil" [Gen. 3:5]). As Roman families prospered, it became fashionable to hire educated Greeks to care for the children. Greek philosophy, with its humanistic and godless base, was soon passed on to the Roman families. Women demanded more rights and, in order to accommodate them, new marriage contracts were designed, including "open marriages."
6. Big Government: By the first century A.D. the father had lost his legal authority. It was delegated to the village, then to the city, then to the state, and finally to the empire. In Rome, citizens complained

about housing shortages, soaring rents, congested traffic, polluted air, crime in the streets, and the high cost of living. Unemployment was a perennial problem. To solve it, the government created a multitude of civil service jobs, including building inspectors, health inspectors, and tax collectors.
7. Decline and Persecution: The problem of big government only multiplied. Meanwhile, a flourishing New Testament Church was established in the Roman Empire through the preaching of the apostle Paul and others. The final act of the Roman Empire was to bring great persecution to these Christians.[5]

Our moral decline hasn't reached these proportions yet by any means. But I think it's important to know where the barbs and hooks of integrity breakdown can lead.

IT'S ONLY NATURAL

Earlier I posed the question, "How did we get this way?" How did we move so much closer to becoming "one nation under greed"? Quite simply. We came by it naturally. "The *natural man* does not receive the things of the Spirit of God," Paul tells us in 1 Corinthians 2:14. "For they are foolishness to him; nor can he know them, because they are spiritually discerned."

Admittedly, it's far easier to hustle the "quick buck" than the "slow cents." And conditions will remain this way until we apply the instruction that Paul adds in the next verse. "But he who is spiritual judges all things" (1 Cor. 2:15).

It is said that about 200 years ago, the tomb of the great conqueror Charlemagne was opened. The sight the workmen saw was startling. There was his body in a sitting position, clothed in the most elaborate of kingly garments, with a scepter in his bony hand. On his knee lay a New Testament passage, with a cold, lifeless finger point-ing to Mark 8:36: "For what shall it profit a man, if he shall gain the whole world, and lose his own soul?"[6]

I also asked at the beginning of this chapter, "What can you and I do to *change* our own methods and motives? How can we earn a lasting profit and judge with the spirit-ual judgment that promotes integrity?"

That question is too profound to answer with a single chapter. More of the answers unfold as we spread out this map of truth in the pages that follow. But for now, join me as we take a few more steps down the sure path of life by . . .

INTEGRITY ACTION PLAN #2

1. Putting God's Word in our hearts. Every time we place our hands over our hearts and pledge, "One nation under God," let's remember to conduct our lives as if we made that statement with our hands on the Bible.
2. Spending our money as if we believed in it. Every coin and every paper currency note reminds us that "In God We Trust."
3. Recognizing the faults of others as personal re-minders to change ourselves.

As we add these steps to those introduced at the end of Chapter 1, they'll give us the renewed confidence we all need to increase our I.Q. (Integrity Quotient). But they may not protect us when what's "Oh, so wrong" seems "Oh, so right." That requires an understanding of the theme in Chapter 3.

3

When "Wrong" Becomes Right

This is an age of mind-numbing paradox. Our country began "with a firm reliance on the protection of Divine Providence." But today it's against the law for children to pray in public school. What seemed right for the preservation of the nation to one generation is now illegal to another.

> "The greatest homage we can
> pay to truth is to use it."
> *Ralph Waldo Emerson*

Why does it seem that one person's delight is another's disgust? How much easier it would be to lead a life of integrity if we could all agree on the definition of "acceptable behavior"! We Christians have a concise package of Ten Commandments. But we also have many times that number of denominations to interpret them for us. So it's little wonder that wherever we look, the windows of truth become layered with semantic and theological fog.

This is an age of mind-numbing paradox. Our country began "with a firm reliance on the protection of Divine Providence." But today it's against the law for children to pray in public school. What seemed right for the preservation of the nation to one generation is now illegal to another.

Recently the state of California paroled a prisoner who was convicted of raping a fifteen-year-old-girl and chopping her arms off below the elbow. Though his victim is now condemned to a lifetime without her hands, Lawrence Singleton served less than ten years in prison. The law released him. Officials have not been able to find a community that wants the man within their city limits. What seems right to the authorities appears wrong to the public.

Here lies the core of integrity. How do we know what's right?

Even the little matters confound us in their own subtle ways. Parents spend two years teaching children how to stand up and speak for themselves. Then they spend another eighteen years teaching them to sit down and be quiet.

"Mind your own business! But remember you are your brother's keeper."

"The early bird gets the worm. But haste makes waste."

"To err is human. But one mistake and you're through."

Life is filled with contradictions. And we don't always resolve them as well as we might.

"FACTS ARE ENEMIES OF THE TRUTH"

Don Quixote makes a humorous remark in the musical, "Man of La Mancha." He used it to hide from the fact that his beloved "Dulcinea" was actually a common barmaid and the dreaded dragon was nothing more than a windmill. When confronted with such "facts," Don Quixote responded, "Facts? Facts are enemies of the truth."

I've heard it said, "You can prove anything from the Bible." True, there are those who would use the facts of scripture to support their own ideas. Satan himself tried this ploy against Jesus. "If You are the Son of God, throw Yourself down (from the pinnacle of the temple where they were standing). For it is written: 'He shall give His angels charge concerning you,' and 'In their hands they shall bear you up, lest you dash your foot against a stone.'" Satan was indeed quoting "the facts of scripture"—Psalm 91—but he was using it as an enemy of the truth. Jesus retorted with another overriding passage, "It is written again, 'You shall not tempt the Lord your God'" (Matt. 4:6–7).

If facts can be enemies of the truth, then it should come as no surprise to you and me that good intentions can be enemies of integrity.

STATISTICALLY MISSPEAKING

Statistics are often used as enemies of the truth. They say statistics never lie. But you find a lot of liars quoting statistics! It's all too easy to leave out data or compare apples with oranges. And once an erroneous statistic is spread around it becomes like toothpaste—virtually impossible to put back into the tube.

Recently I discovered I had fallen victim to a statistical cliché—one that is easy to remember, popular, and wrong. Let me use this occasion to correct a misconception and illustrate once again how "facts" can actually become enemies of the truth.

It's been widely quoted that about one out of two American marriages will end in divorce. This idea is "one of the most specious pieces of statistical nonsense ever perpetrated in modern times," says pollster Louis Harris. Government figures and a recent poll by the Louis Harris Company show that only one in eight marriages will end in divorce. And in any single year, only about 2 percent of existing marriages will break up.[1]

Yes, Census Bureau figures do show about 1.2 million divorces for 2.5 million marriages during an average year. But "one critical element is left out of the equation,"

observes Mr. Harris. "A much, much bigger 52 million
other marriages just keep flowing along like Old Man
River."

This whole episode reminds me of the old adage from
H. L. Mencken: "There is always an easy solution to every
human problem—neat, plausible, and wrong."

EYEWITNESS MYOPIA

Since we have to be cautious about statistics for direction, what can we rely upon to keep us wholehearted,
sound, and unimpaired in character? Surely seeing is
believing?

Maybe.

Elizabeth Loftus is an expert witness who has testified
in hundreds of cases where eyewitness testimony is crucial.
But her experience as a professor of psychology and ad-
junct professor of law at the University of Washington in
Seattle lends little support to the assumption that "seeing
is believing."

"As a psychologist who specializes in memory, I know
that the human mind is subject to distortion," she writes in
an article for *Newsweek* magazine. Loftus informs us,
"People often remember things differently from the way
they really were. And contrary to the popular belief that
traumatic events tend to create an indelible 'fixation' in the
mind, such traumas are often associated with memory
problems. There is, in fact, a body of research challenging
the value of eyewitness memory."[2]

Professor Loftus then summarizes the story of three
innocent citizens who served time in prison because of
erroneous eyewitness testimony. One account involves
a Roman Catholic priest who was falsely identified by
seven witnesses in a series of holdups in Delaware and

Pennsylvania. They swore to tell the whole truth and found it impossible.

THE WAY THAT SEEMS RIGHT

So how reliable is the human mind for control and direction of the life for which it is responsible? How reliable is an umbrella in a hurricane? Scripture leaves little doubt. "There is a way which *seems right* to a man. But its end is the way of *death*" (Prov. 14:12 emphasis mine). Then to reiterate the point, this warning is repeated verbatim by the same inspired author two chapters later in Proverbs 16:25.

"But surely," some may argue, "if I wander around long enough looking for the right answers I'll stumble onto the truth." Unfortunately one of the major prophets takes strong exception to that delusion. "O Lord, I know the way of man is not in himself; it is not in man who walks to direct his own steps" (Jer. 10:23).

The Book of Judges recounts the happenings in Israel when "everyone did what was right in his own eyes" (Judg. 21:25). It was one of the bloodiest eras in their history.

HUMANISM—SPIRIT ANSWERS FROM THE WRONG REALM

To further trouble the waters and muddy the distinction between wrong and righteous, we find ourselves surrounded by the intellectual waves of secular humanism. Here is a philosophy that worships the use of human intellect by rejecting God and canonizing reason as "supreme." Though less obvious than ancient "gods" of wood and stone, such idolatry is equally destructive to integrity.

Secular humanism has its roots in the eighteenth-century "Enlightenment" which taught that man is the master of personal fate and captain of his soul. We see this heresy taking root in the educational system from preschool to postgraduate institutions. But we often overlook its sinister shadow in other circles.

Here are some of the humanistic issues that impair our ability to distinguish right from wrong. These are paraphrased from an article by Donald Bloesch which appeared in *Eternity* magazine.[3]

The ideology of welfare liberalism, which seeks to solve human problems through social engineering, is one manifestation of secular humanism. But the ideology of free enterprise capitalism (classical liberalism), which believes the free market contains all the solutions, is definitely another. Messianic socialism, with its dialectical materialism, is one of the more poisonous fruits of secular humanism.

The Moral Majority, other fundamentalists, and evangelical groups concentrate unduly on the left-wing expressions of these issues. But secular humanism isn't the only pseudoreligious reflection we see in the contorted glass of human reason. Other distortions obscure the path to integrity.

Nationalism

Easy to overlook is the threat of nationalism. This sentiment enthrones the values and traditions of the nation or *Volk* (people). It elevates the national or racial heritage over the autonomous individual (as in classical liberalism) or the political party (as in communism). While secular humanism subverts the family by endorsing sexual freedom, "nationalism" (though posing as the family's defender) subordinates it to the interests of the wider community, the nation-state, which is adorned with a kind of mystical aura.

American fundamentalism has been unable to perceive or appreciate this threat from the political right. This may account for fundamentalism's lack of credibility when it addresses issues that should command the attention of all people of moral sensitivity (including pornography, "value-free" sex education, and abortion).

Technological Materialism

We should also consider the threat to our value system imposed by technological materialism. Jacques Ellul has called this the dominant ideology in modern industrialized nations. According to this world- and life-view, the prime virtues are utility, efficiency, and productivity. People who make no visible contribution to the betterment of society, such as the aged, the retarded, and the severely handicapped, are pushed to one side or even regarded as expendable.

Whereas a great many secular humanists are inner-directed and stress personal integrity, technological materialists are other-directed, emphasizing loyalty to the organization, whether it be the state, corporation, or union. While a significant number of secular humanists prize individuality and freedom, technological materialists encourage the dependence of humanity on technology.

Mysticism

A more subtle challenge to integrity is mysticism—that perennial temptation to turn away from the pursuit of pleasure and power in search of union with the Eternal.

The penetration of Eastern religions into the industrial West has presented a new alternative for tens of thousands of people. Mysticism is usually a world-denying type of philosophy, but some neomystics stress immersion in the world, finding God in the depths of human existence. Whereas secular humanism celebrates the fulfillment of the self, mysticism emphasizes the loss of the self in the collective unconscious, the cosmic process, or the undifferentiated unity.

Mysticism is especially prevalent among those in our churches and theological schools who are intent on recovering spirituality. It is also found among radical feminists, particularly those who are trying to reinstate the nature religion of witchcraft.

Nihilism

Perhaps most sinister of all is the mounting peril of nihilism—the denial of all norms and values. Nihilism is particularly fostered by the technological mentality, which elevates efficiency over ideology and religion. Technocrats try to give technology a rational direction, but the temptation is almost irresistible to sacrifice ends for means. Moreover, a technology without aim or purpose, a soul-less science, is more destructive than constructive. Indeed, the social agenda of nihilism is generally the overthrow of all existing social institutions and all norms. Nihilism ushers in the new barbarians, who are intent on destroying rather than creating, but they destroy in the vain hope that something new and durable will result. The dramatic rise in international terrorism is a manifestation of the unleashing of the spirit of nihilism.

Nihilists, like mystics and occultists, are generally irrationalists, even as secular humanists and technological materialists are supreme rationalists. If the modern age is correctly characterized by what Francis Schaeffer calls "the flight from reason," it seems that nihilism, fascism, and nationalism may be greater threats than secular humanism to behavior and integrity.

WHERE TO TURN?

Since we cannot automatically trust every "ism" and spirit; since we must beware of our own steps and our own mind to determine what is right and what is wrong; since we cannot trust eyewitness testimony and statistics; since we cannot rely upon conventional wisdom of the world around us, where *can* we turn for accurate direction in life? How can anyone be expected to lead a life of integrity if everyone uses different rules? Personally I count it a miracle that modern society can hold together at all with strains such as these tearing at the fabric of its value system.

What this means to you and me in our search for integrity is that we must "prove all things" and "try the spirits" as admonished by the apostle Paul. I'll have a great deal more to say about these matters in Chapter 7 on "New Rules for a New Millennium."

Meanwhile the world is filled with model citizens of dubious loyalty.

WHICH WAY IS NORTH?

Lt. Colonel Oliver North's testimony before the Iran-Contra Congressional committee in Washington in 1987 was an international lesson in contradiction. Here was one of the largest government scandals since the Watergate days of President Nixon—with a "hero" at the helm.

As a Marine Corps officer attached to the National Security Council, North was given the responsibility of carrying out various covert actions in Iran and Nicaragua. Although his assignment at the NSC was originally a desk job, one of his former bosses, Robert McFarlane, described him as "probably the most mission-oriented, can-do professional on the staff."

There is a growing body of evidence that his "can-do" approach "did-do" too much. In 1984 Congress passed a law against spending American dollars on direct military aid to the Nicaraguan resistance fighters, known as the Contras. But there were many highly placed officials in the CIA, State Department, and the NSC who wanted to see those funds continue. Because of his experience in Viet Nam, fighting terrorism, Oliver North was chosen as the ideal person to make this happen.

North soon transformed his office job into the operational assignment he always wanted. Those above him admired his ability to cut through the bureaucracy and get the job done. Those below him simply followed his orders.

North's methods were questionable. Calling upon a former Air Force major who had been denied security clearance and another ex-CIA operative who was convicted of illegally selling munitions to Libya, North assembled a personal supply operation. It was valued at $4 million and included two large transport planes, two medium-sized cargo planes, one single-engine plane, a cargo ship, and a 6,000 ft.-airstrip in Costa Rica. And all this was in addition to multiple millions of dollars North helped attract from third countries and private citizens of the U.S. for use by the Contras.

But all this latitude and innovation raised serious questions. Who authorized him to sell arms to the Iranians and divert the funds to Nicaragua? Was he acting on his

own initiative? Or was he "only following orders"? Add
to this classic dilemma a few smaller allegations about
the personal use of government money, and you have the
recipe for scandal.

As much as his superiors admired the results, they
still held reservations about the methods. One attorney
warned North's new boss, John M. Poindexter: "If you lie
down with dogs, you come up with fleas." Secretary of
State George Shultz was said to view him as a "loose can-
non" whose actions needed to be monitored by the State
Department.[4]

"We've seen an evolution of the image of Col. North
from that of pure patriot to someone who engaged in some
rather petty activities," relates Senator William S. Cohen
of Maine. "The temptations become irresistible. You take a
little for tires, a little for food, a $16,000 gate. The stand-
ards of the private sector start to tarnish the silver on the
public institution. The morals of the marketplace are not
those of the (public) trustees."

But plenty of Americans believed in this faithful soldier with his "Yes, Sir" manner and boyish grin. More than
25,000 individuals voluntarily contributed to the Oliver
North Defense fund, including at least two Congressmen.
His lengthy appearances before congressional investigators
on national TV transformed him into an overnight American folk hero. "Ollie for President" signs cropped up. Everyone seems to have a different idea of what constitutes
integrity in a time of crisis and shifting loyalties.

CONGRESS

Congress may be loud and boisterous when it comes to
investigating the integrity of the President's men, but it
doesn't always make the same noise about its own internal

investigations. In the more secluded recesses of the Capitol, the House Committee on Standards of Official Conduct and the Senate Select Committee on Ethics are investigating allegations of misconduct by its own. At the time of this writing at least five members have been accused of ethical and legal transgressions that make them potential targets for committee investigation. Allegations range from bribery, payroll, and campaign-fund infractions to the possible leaking of classified information to foreign sources.

Despite the 1978 Ethics in Government Act, critics think Congress is too slow to respond; or they shroud their deliberations in silence.

"The problem is, it's very hard for peers to judge peers," says Fred Wertheimer, president of Common Cause. "The system ends up shielding the member; it becomes his protector."[5]

What seems right to the White House is often wrong to Congress. And what seems right to Congress is often wrong to the public. Leaders in power are no different than the rest of us. No matter how much we try to hide our actions, our integrity (or lack of it) always shows through. And there is one critic we can never escape—ourselves. I appreciate the way Edgar Guest drives this point home in his poem . . .

"Myself"

I have to live with myself, and so
I want to be fit for myself to know,
I want to be able, as days go by,
Always to look myself straight in the eye;
I don't want to stand, with the setting sun,
And hate myself for things I have done.

I don't want to keep on a closet shelf
A lot of secrets about myself,
And fool myself, as I come and go,
Into thinking that nobody else will know
The kind of a man I really am;
I don't want to dress up myself in sham.

I want to go out with my head erect,
I want to deserve all men's respect;
But here in the struggle for fame and pelf
I want to be able to like myself.
I don't want to look at myself and know
That I'm bluster and bluff and empty show.

I can never hide myself from me;
I see what others may never see;
I know what others may never know,
I never can fool myself, and so,
Whatever happens, I want to be
Self-respecting and conscience free.[6]

CULTURAL INTEGRITY

We've looked at what happens when wrong seems right in matters of personal integrity. This same inversion can happen in matters of international culture and tradition. Does everything that seems right to the average American appear this way to the rest of the world?

Cultural integrity is a must. For example, in our society it is unthinkable for a man to walk into a church with his hat on and his shoes off. In the Near East it is equally unthinkable for a man to enter a mosque with his shoes on and his hat off!

Even the most unscientific prejudices must be respected. A missionary who does not agree with the teaching of Islam but is working among Moslems must not stop a farmer along the road and ask him about the expected yield of his field. To do so would not be a sign of friendliness as it would in Iowa. Rather, it would be an insult, the equal of calling the man a blasphemer, for "only Allah knows the future."

Some time ago I focused on these differences in an article written for our official *World Vision* publication. I believe the insights still apply: What is there about America—and Americans—that makes us feel superior to our brothers and sisters in Asia—or Africa—or Latin America? I know this is a generalization, but it is too often true to be ignored. This superior attitude creeps out in so many ways that seem innocuous to the offender but are deeply hurtful to the offended. For example, we are apt to call our friends in the national church in Tanzania or Korea or Bolivia the "natives" or "native Christians." Immediately this calls to mind half-naked "savages," headhunters, or illiterate peasants. These are *people*. They would much prefer to be called "nationals" or "national Christians"—or Tanzanians or Koreans or Bolivians. Even when they do not comment on this problem, they cringe inwardly under our patronizing attitude.

Again, this attitude is often reflected in our exported Western-style literature for Christians, with little appreciation or understanding of the culture, ethnic background, and history of the people we seek to reach. It is increasingly important that literature be written and produced by people who have this background.

These people in other cultures are our Christian friends. Although they may carefully note and keenly resent our insensitivities, most would never be so ungracious as to bring them to our attention!

No American traveler abroad would likely admit to

being part of the infamous "ugly American" image. And most are not usually guilty of the gross blunders charged in that term. Yet we are closely observed by Christians in the "younger" churches abroad (in what we so casually call the "mission field" that is *home* to them), and an attitude of condescension too often shows through.

There is no question that the stigma far too often attached to Western missions is a realistic problem which must be faced. Horace Fenton points out this condition: "I believe that the Latin American Mission cannot be really effective in its evangelistic objective until fully rooted in Latin America . . . . There are only a limited number of Latins who will continue to honor us with their membership in our mission unless there are basic and deep changes in our whole structure."[7] Dennis Clark reinforces this view: "It seems almost too late for Western societies to recruit the national because with few exceptions the stigma of being labeled a 'stooge' or 'puppet' reduces usefulness. The more likely pattern of development will be the strengthening of existing missionary societies in Third World nations and proliferations of others."[8]

In discussing this broad topic of international integrity, my friend and associate from World Vision, Tom Houston, tells this story about our clashing system of values.

"In the late sixties, Alan Redpath visited us in Nairobi. He had been seeing Africa only through white missionary eyes. One evening, I invited a group of black leaders to our home to have a meal with him and Marjorie. As he listened to their perspective on the missionary story, he became increasingly frustrated until he burst out and said, 'Did we do nothing right?'

"Then there was a pause, and one man, Daniel Wacko

by name, said, 'Yes, yes. You did do something right. You gave us the standard by which to judge you. If you had not shown us the truth of Christ you would not have put yourself so badly in the dark.'"

WHAT HAVE WE LEARNED?

These experiences remind us it's not enough to live by the integrity that is most comfortable to us personally. We have to stretch our horizons and strive to become "whole and complete" with the pluralistic backgrounds of every klan, kilt, and kin.

We've touched on what I hope have been useful principles in this chapter. Let me highlight them here in our . . .

INTEGRITY ACTION PLAN #3

1. Look for the truth behind the facts.
2. Beware the way that "seems right."
3. Practice shunism. That's the habit of shunning any "ism" or human ideology which separates a person from God.
4. Beware of any hero who isn't seated at the right hand of God.
5. Respect the culture and nationality of all your brothers and sisters on earth.

THE CENTRAL QUESTION

In rehearsing the many strange circumstances throughout this chapter when wrong seems right, we have criss-crossed one central question several times.

How do we know what is right? Certainly we cannot base our final reference for integrity on human reason, "facts," statistics, eyewitness accounts, the way which "seems right," humanism, patriotic heroes, legislators, or international traditions. But where *can* we turn for an accurate guide?

We've seen how Lt. Colonel Oliver North has proven himself, like all men, incapable of pointing out the "true north" of integrity. In Chapter 4 we'll discover the north star of conscience upon which we *can rely* for guidance.

4

Our Mandatory Option

*It's hard to imagine how many times we stake
our lives on the integrity of someone else.
Look at a simple plane flight.*

> "Integrity without knowledge is weak and useless, and knowledge without integrity is dangerous and dreadful."
> *Samuel Johnson*

I enjoy shopping as much as the next person. Take new cars for instance. Here we consider those things that are mandatory for making the car work, and those things that are optional for making it more convenient.

Sometimes it's easy to confuse the two. My family has had this problem upon occasion. It's mandatory that a car have a motor, transmission, and wheels. But it's only optional that the car have eight cylinders, five-speed stick shift, and mag rims. It's mandatory that the car have seats and windows, but leather interior and power features are optional. Now I have nothing against convenience and luxury (within reason). But some people allow their desire for the options to lure them into buying a vehicle whose mandatory functions are inadequate or unsafe. That's like putting the cart before the horsepower.

How often do we do this same thing in our own personal lives? It's easy to mistake our wants for our needs.

And sometimes we even do the opposite. We mistake an urgent need for an expendable want. Such is the case

51

with integrity. Here's something that's mandatory, and many people act as if it is only optional.

Integrity has proven itself to be at the heart and core of survival. Yet why do so many people dismiss it as a mere option they can waive? As we've seen in previous chapters, the result of this oversight can be devastating.

NORTH STAR

Though "star" of his own television appearance before the joint congressional committee, we've seen how Lt. Colonel Oliver North is not the safest indicator of "north" when it comes to the magnetic pole of integrity. But allow me to show you a "north star" of conscience we can always rely upon to supply the mandatory guidance we need in matters of principle and ethics. To see this directional star, we will have to step outside once more into the dark night of sin and confusion where much of the world has lost its way. The more we understand about why integrity is mandatory and not optional, the more we will come to see and trust this north star of conscience.

STAKING OUR LIVES ON INTEGRITY

How should you feel when someone behaves as if the reference point of integrity is only an accessory? In my estimation, words like "frightened," "betrayed," and "incensed" may be too mild.

It's hard to imagine how many times we stake our lives on the integrity of someone else.

Look at a simple plane flight. I do a great deal of traveling, so this is a topic dear to me.

Getting to and from the airport can often be the most dangerous part of the journey. Every car you encounter is

only a matter of inches and milliseconds from plowing into
your vehicle, save for the integrity of each individual
driver. And as I mentioned in Chapter 1, it's been said that
one out of every ten drivers on the road is under the influence of alcohol or some other type of mind-altering chemi-
cal. Their optional adherence to safety is your mandatory
concern.

At the airport, dozens of employees—from the security inspection guards to the maintenance workers to the
air traffic controllers—lay another set of hands on your
well-being. Do they view their training, their daily up-
dates, their timetables as mere options or mandatory re-
sponsibilities?

Once in the air, your life and that of your fellow passengers is in the firm grip of a pilot and his crew. Does this
professional mind the checklists and flight plans as carefully as you mind memos and procedural instructions?
How optional is accuracy and completeness at 600 miles
per hour and 25,000 feet in the air?

But we don't fly every day. Some people never ride
in airplanes. Does that mean we're safe from the integrity
failure of others as long as we keep out of the sky? Obviously not. There are long lists of other professionals who
hold your life in their hands every day—water treatment
technicians, utility workers, toxic waste professionals,
railroad engineers, doctors, and other health care-givers.
What does integrity mean to these people? Thank God
the overwhelming majority of such individuals are dedi-
cated, caring professionals. But unfortunately, we do hear
stories of the railroad engineer on marijuana, the nurse on
morphine, the unscrupulous (or exhausted) doctor, the
mob-controlled toxic waste dump operator, and so on.
Remember it was a safety and training exercise that
caused the Russian error at the Chernobyl nuclear reactor

in 1986. This "accident" sent a cloud of radioactive dust around the world. In this day and age, integrity is not an elective. It is a required subject.

BETRAYED

Events like this remind me of the way I felt when I crushed my hip—pained and betrayed! What once seemed so dependable and permanent turned against me forever at the blink of an eye. My hip had always held up its share of the load until it was destroyed in a grinding head-on collision in 1944. Then followed twenty-four years of pain, limping, and limitations. Fortunately, I was able to have it rebuilt by a marvelous surgeon in 1968—Dr. Otto Aufranc in Boston. But one leg is now shorter than the other, and I have to be careful about placing too much strain on the hip. It can never completely go back to the way it was.

Where once I was confident about the technology of nuclear energy, now I limp along with the uneasy feeling that someone must devote his whole mind to the half-life of nuclear waste for many generations to come.

In a similar manner, I feel betrayed by revelations that the Attorney General of the United States is involved in unethical business dealings. (Whether or not Attorney General Edwin Meese was guilty of arranging special favors for the Wedtech Corporation is a matter for the courts to decide.) In my mind the man is innocent until proven guilty. But there is a definite breakdown of integrity somewhere in the process—even if it's on the side of those who might be accusing him falsely. Nonetheless, I feel betrayed by the simple fact that the highest attorney in the nation is virtually immobilized by questions of morality.

No doubt there are dozens of other issues that evoke similar feelings in other people. The Dalkon contraceptive shield betrayed thousands of women with medical complications. Several decades ago a drug called Thalidomide caused hundreds of expectant mothers in need of sedation throughout their pregnancy to give birth to terribly deformed babies.

HISTORY OF WRONG OPTIONS

How easy it is to lose our way without the knowledge of how to use the north star of conscience. We'll turn the telescope on this heavenly body after we examine a few more earthly examples of people who thought integrity was an option—people from the pages of the Bible.

I start with a man who murdered one fourth of the human race in a single stroke. He cared about himself, but doubted his duties toward anyone else. "Am I my brother's keeper?" asked Cain after clubbing Abel to death. All Cain wanted to do was hold up an offering to God without putting down his feelings of jealousy and envy. In his mind, to change these destructive feelings was only a bothersome option.

Cain had good instruction in treachery. His parents had betrayed more than just a fourth of humanity. They failed the entire human race. God told them, "Of every tree of the garden you may freely eat (enormous options); but of the tree of the knowledge of good and evil you shall not eat (one mandatory requirement)" (Gen. 2:17, 18, additions mine).

But what happened? Adam and Eve mistook the mandatory command for the optional choices. In one simple action, they broke at least half of the Ten Commandments and brought down the death sentence upon themselves and all their progeny. "For in the day that you eat of it, you shall surely die" (Gen. 2:17).

By the way, this verse does not mean that Adam and Eve were to die that very day. But rather it means they would bring themselves under the sure promise of death that very day. God, who inhabits eternity, often speaks of those things that "do not exist as though they did" (Rom. 4:17).

Esau was in line to inherit his father's estate—which included the birthright promise of the holy land. But to him it seemed nothing more than a casual choice. "Soup or salad?" "Dinner or the promised land?" Esau chose dinner and his brother, Jacob, took the promises—all because Esau mistook a mandatory commitment to his heritage as a careless option for the moment. He lost sight of this north star of conscience and crashed into the dangerous rocks of compromise.

Jacob's sons were not immune to this character flaw. In fact, his firstborn son, who should have inherited the birthright, compromised himself and also lost sight of the mandatory option of integrity. "Surely no one expects me to control my passions," he may have reasoned. "I'm the oldest son and next in line to lead this clan. I'll do what I want. And besides, no one will ever find out."

But what happened?

"And it happened, when Israel dwelt in that land, that Reuben went and lay with Bilhah his father's concubine; and Israel heard about it" (Gen. 35:22).

Was the need for moral integrity a mere option in the mind of father Israel (Jacob)? Years later when he was about to die, Jacob gathered his sons around him to confer a final blessing on them. He started with the eldest. "Reuben, you are my firstborn, my might and the beginning of my strength, the excellency of dignity and the excellency of power. Unstable as water, you shall not excel, because you went up to your father's bed; then you defiled it" (Gen. 49:3, 4). Here Reuben discarded a lifetime of favor for himself and his heirs for one short moment of gratification. What appeared to be an optional accessory in life (moral integrity) turned out to be a requirement.

The examples are almost endless.

Moses himself never entered the promised land "Because you did not believe Me, to hallow Me in the eyes of the children of Israel, therefore you shall not bring this congregation into the land which I have given them" (Num. 20:12). Even the small matters of integrity were mandatory.

Two sons of Aaron, the High Priest, died while serving the Holy Tabernacle because they presented "profane fire" to God (Lev. 10:1). Though Samson was imbued with supernatural strength, he died in captivity because of his lust for Philistine women (Judges 16). King Saul lost his chance to become the head of a royal dynasty through self-will (1 Samuel 15). David's sin with Bathsheba, though forgiven by God, resulted in the death of a son, and a blood-filled curse. "You have killed Uriah the Hittite with the sword; you have taken his wife to be your wife, and have killed him with the sword of the people of Ammon. Now therefore, the sword shall never depart from your house, because you have despised Me" (2 Sam. 12:9, 10).

How did David and these other men of the Bible "despise God"? Was it not because they beheld the sacred and called it "profane"?

Centuries later, Judas heard Christ's admonition to become "perfect, just as your Father in heaven is perfect" (Matt. 5:48). But his mind sought another standard. Judas wanted perfect riches. To him sincerity and service were mere options, until this attitude drove him to murder—and suicide.

With so many case histories to learn from, you'd think mankind would comprehend.

But even with the arrival of the Holy Spirit after Christ's ascension into heaven, believers continued to reveal a lack of integrity. Ananias and Sapphira lied to the apostle Peter and paid with their lives (Acts 5:9). Paul laments the state of those who are "turning away so soon from Him who called you in the grace of Christ, to a different gospel" (Gal. 1:6). And John recounts the sad tale of one who is "prating against us with malicious words. And not content with that, he himself does not receive the brethren, and forbids those who wish to, putting them out of the church" (3 John 10).

Centuries later a universal church became so intent on "putting out" the mandatory options of God that one reformer came pounding on the door with hammer and ninety-five theses in hand. In the sixteenth century, Martin Luther's candle against the darkness of optional spirituality kindled a forest fire of mandatory reform which we still feel today as the Protestant Reformation.

Disaster is conceived on a bed of neglect. And God's servants have never been fully celibate in this regard.

SPOTTING THE NORTH STAR

Now that our eyes are adjusted to the evils of the darkness around us in this spiritual night, let's pick out the north star of conscience.

The one thing that characterizes the north star and makes it useful as a celestial point of reference is that it does not move in the sky. Polaris (another name for this sphere) remains fixed while every other star revolves around it during the twelve hours of night. Often you will see a time-lapse photograph of circular streaks around a single fixed star. Here is the unmoving center of a pinwheel that always points north. It's not the brightest spot in the sky, but it is the most reliable.

What point of scriptural truth provides the center for all else to rotate around? What faint axiom gives us the surest guidance?

Is the north star of conscience found in the beatitudes? Here you discover a long passage in Matthew 5 which tells us "blessed are the poor . . . those who mourn, the meek, those who hunger and thirst for righteousness, and those who are persecuted." Excellent admonitions, but this is too large a constellation of revelation to be a single star.

Is it the golden verse of the Bible, John 3:16? "For God so loved the world that He gave His only begotten Son, that whoever believes in Him should not perish but have everlasting life." Superb map, but not a compass.

What verse would you point to?

I realize this is an artificial question. I'm sure there are dozens of passages that might qualify. In fact, the verse I have in mind is a New Testament echo of an Old Testament note. And it's amplified in a parallel scripture fifteen chapters later. But such a mental exercise is good for developing spiritual strength.

For me the north star of conscience is unique. Like polaris, around which circulate all the other stars and heavenly bodies, here is a scripture upon which "hang all the law and the prophets."

You probably guessed this passage and didn't know why. It's called "the Golden Rule": "Whatever you want men to do to you, do also to them, for this is the Law and the Prophets" (Matt. 7:12).

Most people leave off the last clause about "the Law

and the Prophets." But that's what places this verse at the center of the entire Bible.

A parallel passage, which reveals some of the alchemy behind the "golden" aspects of this rule, reflects another facet of this same truth. "You shall love the Lord your God with all your heart, with all your soul, and with all your mind. This is the first and great commandment. And the second is like it: 'You shall love your neighbor as yourself'" (Matt. 22:37–39).

We might not recognize these scriptures as synonymous if it weren't for the next verse. "On these two commandments *hang all the Law and the Prophets*" (v. 40 emphasis mine).

How can there be more than one hook secure enough to hold all the Law and the Prophets? The Golden Rule— "do unto others as you would have them do unto you" (popular paraphrase)—is the same concept as loving your neighbor as yourself. And when you realize that God is our neighbor (who was here in the first place and kind enough to share His front lawn with us newcomers), you understand that the "first and great commandment" is part of the same vein of gold—"You shall love the Lord your God with all your heart, with all your soul, and with all your mind."

What a beautifully simple way to find our direction in the integrity turbulence all around us! All we have to remember is to do unto our neighbor as we would have him do unto us—starting with that first and great neighbor called God.

To my way of thinking, this is a perfect answer to those who seek perfection. But not everyone seeks perfection. And when we do, it's often difficult to get things right even then.

TOO MANY FLOWERS

That reminds me of the man who couldn't even please his lady friend with flowers. A young man was deeply in love with a beautiful girl. One day she told him that the next day would be her birthday, and he laughingly said he would send her a bunch of roses, one for each year of her life.

That evening he wrote to his florist, ordering twenty-four roses to be sent to the young lady on the first delivery the following day. The proprietor of the flower shop, looking over the mail in the morning, said to his salesman:

"Tom, here's an order from young Mr. Higgins for twenty-four roses. He's a mighty good customer; let's give him a break and put in an extra dozen."

The young man never did find out what made his girl friend so angry.

MORAL COMPASS

Even if we're leaning in the right direction, we still need a little support and encouragement to move us along. Over the years I've developed what I like to call a "Christian Survival Compass." Once we find the reference point of north, we still have to understand the importance of south, east, and west.

CHRISTIAN SURVIVAL COMPASS

North—Always keep sight of Christ. As the living Word of God, He reminds us of the "Golden Rule" which embodies "all the Law and the Prophets."

East— Pray. Each sunrise in the east is our reminder to start the day in contact with the Creator.

South—Tackle the problems. We can't run. We've got to face them sometime, somewhere. South of Israel is the great "Negev" desert—the vast wasteland in which the Israelites wandered for forty years because they refused to face their problems. We can hide from people, but not from our troubles.

West— Just as the sun sets in the West, so will our future if we don't control our wandering passions for money, sex, and pride. Paul says, "Let not the sun go down on your wrath" (Eph. 4:26). To which we can add, "Let it not go down on pride, lust, or greed." Flee such vices quickly.

With this counsel controlling our thoughts, we can be confident about the direction and outcome of our lives. For thoughts hold the reins of action. This compass allows us to see clearly. And according to John Ruskin, "To see clearly is poetry, prophecy, and religion, all in one."

What have we seen in this chapter? Let me summarize with . . .

INTEGRITY ACTION PLAN #4

1. Chart your course by the north star of conscience—by doing unto others as you would have them do unto you.
2. Look to the stories about men and women from the Bible to illustrate how small compromises lead to big problems.

3. Build the type of integrity you can stake your life on.
4. Accept the fact that integrity is not optional like wallpaper, but mandatory like the wall.

Looking at the world around us, such suggestions may seem totally unrealistic and unattainable. And if all I had were the examples that command the headlines and dominate the newscasts of late, I'd be inclined to agree with you. But I know these principles can work today and will work tomorrow because they worked so well yesterday. And to prove it, join me in the trophy room for a look at a most amazing "Integrity Showcase."

5

An Integrity Showcase

It's no accident that Billy Graham has appeared on the Gallup Poll's "10 Most Admired Men in the World" listing 26 times in 27 years. His powerful, worldwide ministry has been one of inspiration and integrity from the beginning.

"A good character is the best tombstone. Those who loved you, and were helped by you, will remember you when forget-me-nots are withered. Carve your name on hearts, and not on marble."
Charles H. Spurgeon

I visit many organizations and consequently I see a lot of trophy showcases. You know the ones. Those big, long display cases that are either too full of tarnished trophies or too vacant with lonely ones. But they never fail to grab my attention. Who are all those people on the nameplates? What was the competition like?

Many of those trophies were given to winners of games we've never heard of in the United States. What's "curling"? Seen any "battledore" matches lately? How about "droughts"?

But whenever you look at a gleaming trophy, you know there's a story of struggle and sacrifice—one that turned out well in the end. No matter how long ago the event took place, that trophy still does its job today by motivating the observer to attempt even greater things. And as you struggle to read the event and the name on the medal, you often catch a glimpse of yourself in the reflection. It seems to say, "John Doe was a winner, you can be one too."

Come handle some trophies with me. Pick them up. Read the names. Imagine the struggle and the sacrifice. Then look for your own reflection as well.

But these were not given for athletic prowess, which is often beyond the best of us. Rather, these were given for something else; something we all can attain.

Welcome now to the "Integrity Showcase."

NOBEL PRIZE WINNING MOTHER

Life at the girls' school in India was fulfilling enough until Agnes Bojaxhiu received "the message" in 1946. "Quit the cloistered existence and plunge into Calcutta's slums," it commanded. Thus began a lifelong crusade that earned a Nobel Peace prize in 1979 for the woman who came to be known as Mother Teresa. From collecting abandoned babies out of the garbage to building leprosariums, the *Missionaries of Charity* are committed to serving others "as yourself." The Order operates worldwide with 1800 nuns, 250 brothers, and thousands of co-workers in thirty countries.

What drives Mother Teresa on to award-winning service for Christ despite conditions that would turn the stomach of a hardened streetfighter? "For me each one is an individual," she once explained. "It is not social work. We must love each other. It involves emotional involvement, making people feel they are wanted."[1]

In her latest book, Mother Teresa takes an even deeper look at the championship heart of these "Angels of Mercy": "The Missionaries of Charity are not social activists but contemplatives in the very heart of today's world. We take literally the words of Jesus: 'I was hungry, I was naked, without a home, and you gave me food, you clothed me, you gave me shelter' (see Matt. 25:35–36). In this way we are in contact with Him 24-hours a day. This contemplation, this touching of Christ in the poor, is beautiful, very real, and full of love."[2]

This explanation gives me even greater appreciation for some stirring words by Mother Teresa I read a number of years ago. Simple, yet profound, they certainly belong in our integrity showcase.

> When I was homeless, you opened your doors,
> When I was naked, you gave me your coat,
>
> When I was weary, you helped me find rest,
> When I was anxious, you calmed all my fears,
>
> When I was little, you taught me to read,
> When I was lonely, you gave me your love,
>
> When in a prison, you came to my cell,
> When on sick bed, you cared for my needs,
>
> In a strange country, you made me at home,
> Seeking employment, you found me a job,
>
> Hurt in a battle, you bound up my wounds,
> Searching for kindness, you held out your hand,
>
> When I was Negro, or Chinese, or White,
> Mocked and insulted you carried my cross,
>
> When I was aged, you bothered to smile,
> When I was restless, you listened and cared,
>
> You saw me covered with spittle and blood,
> You knew my features, though grimy with sweat,

When I was laughed at, you stood by my side,
When I was happy, you shared in my joy.[3]

BEACON OF INTEGRITY

Our next souvenir in the showcase of integrity is a close personal friend of mine. I could write an entire book about his accomplishments. But then, that would be the "teacup calling the pitcher 'crystal'" (to reverse an old adage about pots and kettles). More believable are the words of a hardened newspaper publisher. The following editorial appeared in the *Miami Herald* on 12 April 1987, a Sunday edition. Written by the publisher, Dick Capen, these words stand as a glowing tribute to Christian Integrity.

BILLY GRAHAM: BEACON OF INTEGRITY
A man who lacks judgment derides his neighbor,
but a man of understanding holds his tongue.
—Proverbs 11:12
There is a time for everything . . .
a time to be silent and a time to speak.
—Ecclesiastes
In recent weeks, television evangelists . . . have provided fresh fodder for those who delight in cutting others to pieces. Critics are quick to condemn and slow to forgive. It's an ugly scene.
Amid this swirl of controversy, the most respected evangelist of our time—the Rev. Billy Graham—has kept quiet. So far, he has turned down 140 media requests for interviews. To me, his message of silence has been as powerful as 100 sermons. While clearly pained by the serious mistakes of others, Dr. Graham has refused to allow the sins of a few to overshadow the important work of his Christian mission. "God's work is so much greater than

these troubles," Dr. Graham told me while preparing for his next crusade.

In a March 1983 *TV Guide* cover story, Dr. Graham warned of the dangers of mixing money and politics with televised religion. An opponent of heavy-handed tactics for raising money from TV viewers, he founded the Evangelical Council for Financial Accountability (ECFA) to promote annual audits and open financial records.

It's no accident that Dr. Graham has appeared on the Gallup Poll's "10 most admired men in the world" listing 26 times in 27 years. His powerful, worldwide ministry has been one of inspiration and integrity from the beginning.

Dr. Graham considers television to be an extension of his ministry, not the essence of it. Each year his crusades are rebroadcast over 330 TV stations during prime evening hours, and they generate a tremendous interest. Last month's televised crusade, for example, generated more than 400,000 letters, with a record 137,000 received in one day.

Since the first crusade in 1947, more than 107 million people have gone to hear Dr. Graham. He's preached the gospel to more people in person than anyone else in history. On two occasions, one million people attended a single day's session. Both meetings were in Seoul, Korea. Crusades have been held in 46 states and in 64 countries. This summer, Dr. Graham will complete the 50-state circuit.

For 36 years the Graham family has lived in a modest North Carolina mountain home built on land they purchased for $12 per acre. The 68-year-old Graham and his wife, Ruth, have five grown children and 18 grandchildren. Dr. Graham drives a 1977 Oldsmobile. His current salary, which is set by the BGEA board, is $69,000 a year. All money raised through the evangelist's worldwide ministry goes directly to the BGEA in support of the group's extensive programs.

Despite the overwhelming success of his ministry, Dr. Graham remains humble about the impact of his life's work. To him, reaching more than 100 million people is "a drop in the bucket," given the world's population. "All I want," Rev. Graham says, "is to be remembered as a simple proclaimer of the gospel of Christ. I want people to think of me as a person who walked in His integrity."

Sin has been around for a long time, and no one is immune from its reach. March may have been a disastrous month for some TV evangelists, but the dynamic and inspiring ministry of Billy Graham continues to soar. "The church has lived through these things for centuries," he said. "How the Lord has ever put up with His church, I'll never know."[4]

There's one thing we can be sure of, the Lord and the world have little trouble "putting up with" people who walk in "His integrity." This kind of example deserves a permanent memento in our showcase.

PRAYERS VS. BULLETS

But you don't have to be a Christian superstar to earn a mark in the record book of life. I enjoy this story from a friend and supporter of World Vision.

D-Day, 1944—Though unarmed, he led a boatload of troops into battle on Omaha beach. They had rifles, but all he carried was the sword of the Word. Captain George R. Barber, a longtime friend of World Vision and myself, tells a fascinating story about his experiences as an Army Chaplain during World War II. When you think about it, the only thing standing between a military Chaplain and a casket is integrity.

They don't draft ministers, you have to volunteer. Russell Barber (he uses his middle name in civilian life) enlisted in October of 1941 and was sent for training at a Horse Cavalry division in El Centro, California. "Have you ever ridden a horse before?" asked the officer in charge. "No," replied Russell. "Well, that's no problem. The horse we got for you has never had a rider before either. You'll get along just fine." But it didn't take the Army long to realize that cavalry divisions weren't going to be much good in this conflict. They soon transferred the chaplain to armored and artillery divisions.

As a chaplain, George R. Barber (they used his actual first name in the military) was trained to conduct himself as an officer. This proved to be more than a formality on the blood-stained beach called "Omaha" in Europe. After scrambling down the side of a troop ship with the other soldiers on 6 June 1944, Captain Barber discovered that he was the only officer on board a landing boat filled with thirty infantrymen. Casualties were heavy all around them. Nearby a direct hit from German artillery extinguished thirty souls. When his craft landed, Captain Barber realized that he was in command of this landing party. Armed only with a prayer, he led his men into the face of lesser equipped enemies.

On that one beach, 1,531 men died. But their sacrifice helped advance 50,000 other Allied troops toward victory. During that campaign, Captain Barber spent eleven months and three days serving the spiritual needs of big Red One, the Army's First Armored Division. Those needs included the proper Christian burial of 7,000 young men. And the Christian encouragement of thousands more.

At the Fortieth Anniversary commemoration of these events in Europe in 1984, George revisited all these same spots from Omaha to Czechoslovakia and "had a good cry for the men."

Not long after the war George Barber was recalled for active duty in Korea. After the hostilities simmered down in the mid '50s, he was walking the streets of Seoul with the founder of World Vision, Rev. Bob Pierce. There they encountered a heartrending sight. Wandering the streets of that one city were 100,000 orphans. Proverbs tells us

that Wisdom "raises her voice in the open squares" (Prov.
1:20). Here she was screaming and kicking as well. What
do you say to 100,000 orphans who do not speak your
language (yet long to hear the universal syllables of love)?
How would a man of integrity react? Would he turn his
back and move on to the selfish pleasures? Or would he roll
up his sleeves with a comrade and answer the voice of
Wisdom? George Barber chose to encourage Bob Pierce in
a long-lasting child care program in Korea.

Today as a retired Lt. Colonel in the Air Force, George
R. Barber often takes the opportunity to address clubs and
civic groups. He tells his story and leaves the audience with
a simple reminder. Jesus sought to go about doing good.
Most people today seek to go about doing. We can choose
which example to follow. And somehow that choice seems
easier with men like George Barber around us still.

However—I'll be among the first to confess that you
have to beware of some of the saints you encounter. There's
a story going around about an elderly lady who rented a
room to two boys whom she did not know. At first she was
worried, but soon she stopped fretting. She discovered, so
she told a neighbor, that they were nice boys. "They must
be nice," she explained to her friend, "because they have
lots of towels from the Young Men's Christian Association in
their room."

All that glitters is not gold.

TIMBUKTU

I'll never forget my friend Pastor Nauck in Timbuktu,
Mali. He is the oldest son of one of his father's seven wives.
He grew up in the stark, arid Sahara desert. Yet at the age

of twelve he was converted to Christianity by a visiting missionary evangelist—despite the fact that his father was a Muslim. When the boy reached the age of eighteen, this same evangelist arranged for him to attend Bible school in the capital city of Bamako. That gave him every reason and opportunity to leave his vacant homeland. But he didn't. Instead he set his hand to gather a small flock for Jesus; thirty men, plus women and children. When I talked with him several years ago, he said, "I never intend to leave here. This is where God has called me." Where once there were no Christians at all, now there is a congregation of thirty men who go out and visit the Taureg tribespeople. I helped arrange for World Vision International to buy him a donkey. Now he can ride across the sand to make his visits instead of walking.

To me, this is a compelling example of integrity. This dear brother could easily go to some other African region with more comforts. But he decided to stay in the toughest place possible, Timbuktu. A young man about thirty-five years old, Pastor Nauck looks forward to a long life of service ahead through integrity.

"My Ball Moved"

Most of the trophies you see in a showcase come from victories in sports. And it's often easy to assume that these games are filled with selfish attitudes and cutthroat competitiveness. But I find it encouraging to know that many players score as well in integrity as they do in points.

I enjoy the game of golf and sometimes do pretty well. But when my scorecard starts to resemble a bowling game, I remind myself that I'm first a Christian, then a golfer.

That makes me feel better until I read examples like this. Here's a good Christian *and* a good golfer. This example is taken from a book by Cliff C. Jones entitled, *Winning through Integrity*:

Sports writers have often referred to Tom Watson as the greatest golfer in the world. He has won nearly every major golf tournament at least once and many of them several times. Fame and fortune have not spoiled him. He is respected as well as admired by all who have followed his outstanding career.

Both his skill and integrity were evident at an early age. He had his heart set on becoming a champion. He also had his personal code of honor firmly in mind. In the first state tournament that he ever entered, he put his putter down behind his ball on one of the greens. To his dismay, the ball moved slightly. No one saw it. Of that he was certain. He was under great pressure to win, and there was no time whatever to add up the pluses and minuses of the alternatives. But he knew without hesitation what he must do; he went over to an official and said, "My ball moved." That action cost him a stroke, and he lost the hole. Tom Watson placed his personal integrity ahead of his keen desire to win.

Happily, as it turned out, he did succeed in winning the match. He came back to win that particular state tournament three more times. He has gone on to win world championships, fame, international respect, and lives a truly happy life with an unblemished conscience.

As Jesus so truly promised, "But seek first [God's] kingdom and his righteousness, and all these things shall be yours as well (Matthew 6:33)."[5]

THE GENTLE GIANT

Golf is a gentle game, played mostly by gentlemen and women. You'd expect it to invite integrity. But what about some of the more aggressive sports—like football?

Here's an inspirational "trophy" from *Possibilities* magazine:

Roosevelt Grier overwhelms people. Maybe it's because of his six-foot-six, three-hundred-pound build that helped the Los Angeles Rams football team become NFL champions in the early sixties. Or perhaps it's knowing that he spent a weekend with President Carter in the White House, starred in his own TV show, campaigned with Bobby Kennedy, or even (more recently) wrote his own autobiography, *Rosey: The Gentle Giant* (Harrison House Publishers).

But mostly this son of a Georgia farmer overwhelms people with love. "Life is a team concept," says Rosey, and throughout his fifty-three years of mistakes and success, he has strived to meet others' needs in a spirit of love.

This attitude has been most evident in times of crisis. When Bobby Kennedy was shot in 1968, Rosey wrestled assassin Sirhan Sirhan to the ground and took his gun, at the same time protecting him from a crowd angry enough to kill him. Today Rosey and his wife Margie apply their love and determination in educating and equipping young kids in Los Angeles' inner city to become independent, productive adults.[6]

Rosey's organization is called "Are You Committed?" His life is a positive answer to that question. As a close personal friend, I've seen Rosey pitch in as an ambassador to black America and rally thousands of young people to help the starving masses in Africa. This gentle giant has awesome power—through integrity.

PEOPLE NEVER FORGET WHAT YOU'RE MADE OF

It started out as a small, insignificant story—until the *New York Times* picked it up as a front page, human interest feature. During the height of so many ugly disclosures we have presented in earlier chapters about shattered character, this beautiful example of wholehearted integrity caught the eye of millions of people:

For Town and Team, Honor Is Its Own Reward

CONYERS, Ga.—For Coach Cleveland Stroud and the Bulldogs of Rockdale County High School, it was their championship season: 21 wins and 5 losses on the way to the Georgia boys' basketball tournament last March, then a dramatic come-from-behind victory in the state finals.

But now the new glass trophy case outside the high school gymnasium is bare. Earlier this month the Georgia High School Association deprived Rockdale County of the championship after school officials said that a player who was scholastically ineligible had played 45 seconds in the first of the school's five postseason games.

You Got to Do What's Honest

"We didn't know he was ineligible at the time, we didn't know it until a few weeks ago," Mr. Stroud said. "Some people have said we should have just kept quiet about it, that it was just 45 seconds and the player wasn't an impact player.

"But you got to do what's honest and right and what the rules say. I told my team that people forget the scores of basketball games; they don't ever forget what you're made of."

The town (of about 8,000 people 25 miles east of Atlanta) has rallied behind the school and the coach, just as they did when the team was winning and Conyers was on a roll. Even though they know it cost the school the title, many people here say they support the decision to admit the violation, rather than try to cover it up.

"We have scandals in Washington and cheating on Wall Street," wrote Vicki and Bill Ball, in a letter to *The Rockdale Citizen* last week. "Thank goodness we live in Rockdale County, where honor and integrity are alive and being practiced."

In fact, when the newspapers solicited a few hundred dollars in contributions to buy the school a new trophy to replace the one the state wants returned, and medallions for each of the players to commemorate their winning season, the paper raised so much money it had to send some back.[7]

Here the lasting benefits of integrity certainly outweighed the short-term glory of a single state championship. Had the Rockdale Bulldogs kept the trophy, they would have been recognized in Georgia. But they would also have risked exposure to a major scandal. This way they made the front page of a national newspaper, and the pages of this book (and no telling how many other journals and magazines) because of their "bulldog" tenacity for integrity. Hats off to Coach Cleveland Stroud and the entire Rockdale County High School.

MIRACLE AT PHILADELPHIA

As I write these chapters about the ragged teeth of irresponsibility that could saw a nation in half, the United States of America is celebrating the two hundredth anniversary of the document that has bound this country together. Two centuries ago in Philadelphia, the architects of the U.S. Constitution reviewed the "integrity of the ages" to provide the foundation and superstructure for the government of the new world. Their humble acceptance of enduring values created the most stable government on earth today and the longest running democratic society.

The influence of this document is discernible in nearly all national constitutions in force today. Poland and France framed their original constitutions in 1791, four years after the United States. One hundred fifty-nine other nations followed suit.

Both George Washington and James Madison, who participated in the heated debates May 25 through July 17, 1787, called the constitution a "Miracle."

I can believe such an observation when I read words like these which Benjamin Franklin addressed to George Washington, presiding officer of the convention. "How has it happened, Sir, that we have not hitherto once thought of humbly applying to the Father of lights to illuminate our understandings? If a sparrow cannot fall to the ground unseen by Him, is it probable an empire could arise without His aid?"[8]

The delegates agreed that "on the approaching Fourth of July a sermon be preached at the request of the Convention and that thenceforth prayers be used."[9]

Who could place a price tag on this one single act of integrity?

HONEST ABE

Our patriotic showcase would not be complete without a place for Abraham Lincoln. Do we recognize him as a man of conviction because he helped save our nation during the Civil War? Or did he steer us through those treacherous waters because he was already a man of integrity?

Here's a small story you may not have heard which further illustrates the depth of this man's convictions.

At the age of twenty-four, Abraham Lincoln served as the postmaster of New Salem, Illinois, for which he was paid an annual salary of $55.70.

Even then, twenty-four years before he entered the White House, the rail-splitter was showing the character that earned him the title of "Honest Abe."

The New Salem post office was closed in 1836, but it was several years before an agent arrived from Washington to settle accounts with ex-postmaster Lincoln, who was a struggling lawyer not doing very well.

The agent informed him that $17 was due the government. Lincoln crossed the room, opened an old trunk and took out a yellowed cotton rag, bound with string. Untying it, he spread out the cloth and there was the $17. He had been holding it untouched for all these years.

"I never use any man's money but my own," he said.[10]

THE VOICE OF DISSENT

To look at someone more contemporary, I have always admired the example of my friend Senator Mark Hatfield of Oregon. During the dark days of Viet Nam when most of his Republican colleagues were calling for escalation of the war, Senator Hatfield stood by his convictions. To him, the war was wrong, and U.S. participation in it a nightmare. Because of the integrity of his stand, he lost friends and became the target of numerous attempts at character assassination. Today, the issues which Senator Hatfield defended during that war are remembered by only a few whereas the *integrity* of his conscience continues to shine as a beacon for all.

Because of Senator Hatfield's uncompromising integrity, I considered it an honor when he agreed to write the foreword for my book, *The Pursuit of Excellence*.[11] In my mind, excellence and integrity go hand in hand.

CLOUD OF WITNESSES

When reviewing a showcase of integrity, it would be impossible to pass by without noticing "so great a cloud of witnesses" which the apostle Paul singled out for admiration in Hebrews 11, the "faith" chapter. But since he tells the stories with such enduring clarity; and since we've been covering these personalities throughout our discussion (and will continue to do so in the remaining chapters), I will defer to the apostle by inviting you to read his catalog of character in Hebrews 11.

But let me hasten to add, without such inspired examples we would not have any real knowledge of or appreciation for this yardstick called integrity.

We've seen many different trophies during this showcase review. Some remind me of cups and plaques. Others seem like certificates, ribbons, or antlers on the wall. But all of them reflect the qualities that can save you and me from untold heartache.

INTEGRITY ACTION PLAN #5

1. Look for the good example in others and follow it.
2. Take care of what you're made of; people never forget.
3. Live your life as though it were a tribute to someone else.

The apostle Paul speaks of the ultimate trophy. "And everyone who competes for the prize is temperate in all things. Now they do it to obtain a perishable crown, but we for an imperishable crown" (1 Cor. 9:25). May your showcase be adorned with such a lasting honor—because we all need as much encouragement as possible to face the realities of Chapter 6.

6

Head of Gold,
Feet of Clay

We have a great relationship today. But it could have come a lot sooner had I expressed more integrity toward the needs of my family.

> "When wealth is lost, nothing is lost;
> When health is lost, something is lost;
> When character is lost, all is lost."
> *Anonymous*

The prophet Daniel received the vision of a mysterious, towering statue. Its message was a voice of prophecy. But its symbolism also speaks of integrity. Through a dream, Daniel saw a kingly figure with head of gold, arms of silver, belly of brass, legs of iron, and feet of clay (Dan. 2:32, 33). It represented successive governments down through history that deteriorated in character from gold to clay over the course of centuries.

But there's more to this image than obscure prophecy. To my way of thinking, its message touches the everyday life of us all. Here is a graphic reminder that the natural condition of humankind (no matter how opulent) stands precariously balanced upon two feet of clay.

Like that statue, our heads are filled with ideas of gold. The intentions of our hearts are as pure as silver. The "fire in our belly" rages in a furnace of brass. Our legs propel us upon pillars of iron. But the image is neither complete nor sound with integrity. For in the natural (unconverted) state, we pile the weight of all these treasures onto feet of brittle clay.

87

This vision is a warning to pagans and Christians alike. All of us are potentially lame. We dare not be too quick to point the finger at others, or too eager to brag on our own accomplishments. "Wherefore let him that thinks he stands take heed," warned the apostle Paul, "lest he fall" (1 Cor. 10:12). The head of gold is never too far from a sole of mud.

Earlier in this book I promised a "sinner's scrapbook" of Ted W. Engstrom. As much as I would enjoy confining the material in these pages to a list of other people's mistakes, I recognize the importance of marching out my own misdeeds for review as well. Somehow, for all of us, gasping in horror at the mistakes of others makes it easier to breathe out the confession of our own shortcomings. The result, in an atmosphere of Christian concern, is long-term improvement.

So with stories both pleasant and painful, let the improvement begin.

"WHERE'S DAD?"

How can you place a value on the importance of time with your family? During the early years of my ministry, I was away from home much of the time, preaching to teenagers, ministering across the world. So time with the family was always special. I tried to enhance those golden moments with nightly phone calls from faraway cities and countries. My returns, though I may have been gone for only a few days, or for several weeks, amounted to midseason Christmases. I always came home laden with gifts: dolls from all over the world for JoAnn, and carefully selected presents for the boys and Dorothy.

Nevertheless, by the time Gordon, my oldest, became active in high school sports, he was troubled by these frequent absences. "Dad," he gently reminded me one day, "you haven't seen me play many of our games, have you?"

That was a real conscience javelin. I immediately pulled out my datebook and circled every football game, home and away, Gordon would play the next season, his senior year. And I'm pleased to say that I attended every one of them. Gordie was ecstatic! But how can we ever make up for those lost, formative years?

It's difficult to express the emotions Dorothy and I felt when we received news some years later that our twenty-year-old son was using marijuana. Those were some pretty tough days. And I'm not proud to say it happened in my family. But I am pleased to say that Gordon gave me cause to reevaluate and strengthen a number of important values. We have a great relationship today. But it could have come a lot sooner had I expressed more integrity toward the needs of my family.

PENNIES FROM HEAVEN

But then what do you expect from a Sunday School thief?

During my rather turbulent high school years, despite the fact that I was not a professing Christian, I was elected president of the Young People's Society of the East Side Alliance Church, as well as Sunday school treasurer. And since I was always in need of money, I started taking advantage of this latter position and began pocketing a quarter or more every time I counted the Sunday school offering.

But I never actually forgot the numerous quarters and dimes I "borrowed" from the Sunday school offering. So, following my conversion as a college freshman, when Jesus spoke to my conscience, I was not surprised. "You've got to make restitution for that money you stole," the Lord reminded me.

"I will," I promised with resignation.

"When?"

"Right away," I responded. And that meant I had to speak to the Sunday school superintendent about the matter.

Ralph Gibson was a giant of a man, towering six feet, six inches. He loved the Lord, and though he projected a very tough exterior, he was a warm-hearted soul. With the icy chills that ran down my back, however, I hardly recognized those qualities of warmth and compassion.

One Sunday I stopped him. Quaking inside and out, I said, "Mr. Gibson, may I see you right after the service?"

"Of course, Ted," he boomed.

I was so fearful of our meeting that I scarcely got anything out of the service. When the crowd finally left, I approached the dreaded superintendent. Gibson smiled warmly and said, "You wanted to talk to me . . . ?"

"Yes, sir," I began, with my heart where the Adam's apple belongs. "I've got something to tell you. Mr. Gibson, when I was Sunday school treasurer, I stole some money from the offering."

There! I'd done it. I had managed to confess my sins.

Gibson looked me straight in the eye, his face a mixture of warmth and sternness. He didn't speak immediately. Then he asked softly, "Well, Ted, what are you going to do about it?"

"Well, I'm going to pay it back. I don't have any money now. But I'll pay it back as best as I can."

"Of course you will," Gibson said. "You must do that."

He thought for a moment. "Let me tell you something," he said. "You pay back what you think you have stolen . . . that's very important. Give it to me and I'll put it in the Sunday school treasury. And only three of us will know about this . . ."

"Three?" I responded.

Gibson smiled. "Yes. You and I. And God. Nobody else will ever know."

It took me all summer to pay off that unrecorded note. I'm sure I returned far more money than I lifted. But when that score was finally settled, I sure had much more respect for the value of honesty and integrity.

PAY THE DRIVER

Probably a good half—maybe more—of life's lessons are difficult for you and me.

One of two women riding on a bus suddenly realized she hadn't paid her fare. "I'll go right up and pay it," she declared.

"Why bother?" her friend replied. "You got away with it—so what?"

"I've found that honesty always pays," the other said virtuously, and went up to pay the driver.

"See, I told you honesty pays!" she said when she returned. "I handed the driver a quarter and he gave me change for fifty cents."

TRANSPARENT LIVES

This matter of integrity is far more than dollars and cents; it's more than lying or cheating. It speaks to the need for transparency in our lives. Certainly all of us, if we will admit it, are tempted to fudge on income tax reporting or other expense records. But what about the other temptations?

What happens in your hotel room when you can spend $5.25 to view a pornographic movie without getting "caught"? Is that integrity? There's the matter of playing "footsy" with the opposite sex. I knew a "brother" who would say, "Let me pray for you, sister (in my office)" and insist on wrapping sister in his arms as he prayed. How impressed was God?

I have a dear friend who is now in heaven. He would sneak off after a meal to get a smoke. When nobody was watching him on an airplane, he would order his after-dinner cocktail while traveling to deliver a message about the evils of sin and drink. He was a strong Christian leader. But how many accomplishments of the spirit did he drive away with the clink of a glass or a tap on an ashtray?

We can easily condemn such obvious lack of integrity. But what about our refined indiscretions? It's equally dishonest to preach on the value of a quiet time when you've never done it yourself. It's dishonest to talk about the power of prayer and lead a prayerless life. Isn't it dishonest to talk about forgiveness and fail to forgive? I think you'd agree that it's dishonest to practice sin and preach righteousness.

Solomon warned us about the little foxes that spoil the vine. Once you make the first compromise, it's easy to make the second, then the third, then the next, and the next . . . .

When do we outgrow temptation? I asked Dr. Paul Rees, 87 years young and one of my heroes, "Paul, you're a veteran of the cross, and a noble gentleman with an impeccable reputation. Are you ever tempted?" He replied, "I'm constantly tempted. At my age, I'm continually tempted." It encouraged me to know a man of his stature who was willing to admit the longevity of temptation. Misery loves company and so does temptation. (You'll read of the libido of another octogenarian in a few pages.)

Integrity is a willingness to admit the problem and seek the Lord's help in time of weakness. What problems do you and I still need to admit?

I'll confess there are a few dogs still nipping at the heels of my conscience.

Too often it seems I pour out so much energy preaching a "great" message I don't have any strength left over to put it into practice. For example, my devotional life. I talk to people all the time about the importance of studying the Word and often find myself neglecting it. Then there's the power of prayer. I have a message about:

God's four answers to prayer
1. No, not yet;
2. No, I love you too much;
3. Yes, I'm glad you asked;
4. Yes, and there's more to come.

It's a great message. I believe it and preach it with effectiveness, but I don't always practice what I preach.

It's my prayer that my willingness to admit these weaknesses will keep moving me closer to a solution.

WHEN CLAY FEET CRUMBLE

Today's crop of errant televangelists and ministers are not the only ones to fall into the lap of lustfulness. Nor will they be the last. The shame of a well-known television evangelist is no more crushing than that of a local pastor who disappoints the local congregation. Just because we haven't heard of a scandal this week doesn't mean that several congregations across the land aren't wrestling with another "incident" this very day. It can happen almost anywhere.

Here are seven points to keep in mind about spiritual leaders who fall. They are taken from the June 1987 issue of *Moody Monthly* magazine. They are so good they bear repeating here.

1. *Churches have a right to expect their leaders to be "above reproach."* This is the first biblical requirement of a local church overseer (1 Tim. 3:2).

Scripture requires such conduct for good reason. It affirms that a man and his message are inseparably connected. To lose faith in one is to lose faith in the other. Paul told the Corinthians: "Follow my example, as I follow the example of Christ" (1 Cor. 11:1). Christian truth is learned through relationships. When we see it come alive in others, we believe we can make it work in us.

2. *Because Christian leaders are creatures of flesh, our expectations for them must be realistic.* When candidate Jimmy Carter admitted he sometimes had impure thoughts about women, it caused a minor national scandal. It shouldn't have; he was only saying the obvious.

Every church leader struggles with impure thoughts. My own pastor once told me he was afraid to go to the beach because the girls were so scantily dressed. He was 83 years old! Many times I have found comfort in the psalmist's honesty. David, recognizing his vulnerability, prayed continually: "Test me and know my anxious thoughts" (Ps. 139:23).

Congregations are setting themselves up for a fall if they will not permit their leaders to admit their humanness. Have churches unwittingly adopted the attitude that "pastors must be perfect; we can remain sinners"?

3. *Placing leaders on pedestals, we tempt them to entertain thought of special privilege.* In a recent counseling session, a couple's problems stemmed from the husband's subconscious feeling that because of his demanding

occupation he was "entitled" to certain sexual outlets that were off limits to ordinary people.

Church leaders are not immune to such reasoning. Whether it entails visiting women at night, counseling behind closed doors, or engaging in too much physical contact, all may attempt to be justified in the name of ministry.

A variation on this theme is for a leader to deny vulnerability: "God has called me into His service, and I am unaffected by such temptations!" Nonsense. The sensitive personality of most pastors I know renders them more vulnerable.

4. *Christian leaders who fall into sin should be treated like any believer who is caught in serious sin.* Two facts stand out.

First, the goal of all church discipline is restoration. The Bible teaches that Scripture is useful for "correcting," which implies "restoration to an upright state" (2 Tim. 3:16). By the outworking of the love of Christ, a congregation's bitterness and sense of betrayal can be turned into a genuine desire to see a sinning brother rediscover the beauty of holiness.

Second, Scripture clearly teaches a pattern for discipline. As you study Matthew 18:15–20, consider its many implications for consistent action:

—It speaks of a "brother." Discipline is a family matter. We have a responsibility to one of our own.

—It commands us to "go." Though most of us hate confrontation, Scripture demands it. We must discover the real story firsthand.

—It tells us the confrontation should be "just between the two of you." Most sin need not become a public scandal.

—It tells us to "show him his fault" or "reprove him" (NASB). Don Baker (of the Hinson Memorial Baptist Church in Portland, Oregon—where a member of his staff was discovered to have been unfaithful to his wife with at least ten other women from three churches) defines this as "the gentle, loving word of warning that tells the offender that someone knows and cares about the sin in his life."

—It seeks restoration: "If he listens to you, you have won your brother over" (NIV).

—It clarifies the alternative: "But if he will not listen." When reproof is rejected, privacy gives way to public action.

—It explains the role of the church: "Tell it to the church." It is the believer's final court of appeals. But if someone rejects the church's directive, public censure gives way to expulsion. "Treat him as you would a pagan or a tax collector." This refers to excommunication—being put out of the worshiping community.

5. *There are appropriate and inappropriate ways for church members to work through their feelings.* To avoid gossip, the two congregations I described (in an earlier portion of this same article) were informed by a trusted authority.

Neither congregational meeting degenerated into a free-for-all for venting frustrations. An authority asked people to pray about their feelings and search out the reasons for their anger. They were invited to talk to a staff member. They were warned against becoming judgmental or bitter. But they were also apprised of the seriousness of the problem and the difficulties in seeking complete restoration. They were urged to pray.

Finally, they were admonished not to permit the enemy to gain an advantage through their attitudes toward the sinner, the church's leaders, or those who took a softer or harder line. If one sensed such feelings in another, he was encouraged to reach out to him, perhaps by studying together Galatians 6:1–5.

6. *It is never easy to restore faith in leaders who fall into sexual sin.* At the beginning of the counseling process, Baker asked Greg's (not his real name) psychologist, "What are the prospects for complete recovery?" He replied, "Very poor. It's seldom that one ever is able to be completely freed from this lifestyle when it has been allowed to become so ingrained in his being."

7. *Because reputation is so central to effective ministry, some who fall into sin will never again be extended the trust necessary to lead.* Unlike Baker's, many congregations would have denied reordination to a fallen pastor under any circumstances.

Apart from genuine trust, no ministry can succeed. And in many situations, trust once betrayed will not be restored. Yet we dare not minimize what God can do.

The church can do more than sit in despair, waiting for news of the next leader to fall. We can uphold our spiritual leaders in daily prayer. May every Christian leader understand the devastating consequences that sinful behavior might bring to his family, his ministry, his congregation, and his Lord.[1]

ALL SENTENCE, NO TRIAL

These are extremely practical suggestions. In fact, I should have used them myself several years ago when I received word of a well-known man in Christian circles who was being accused of homosexuality. The rumors were flying of his sexual exploits both at home and abroad. No one had yet proved anything, but it seemed as if the allegations had every reason to be verified as truth. I believed them, and when I finally invited the man into my office, I unloaded both barrels. I judged him, and spoke harshly. I was so relentless in my attack that he quickly found himself painted into a corner from which there was no possible escape.

I was so certain I had judged him correctly that I didn't bother to listen to him. I knew I was right, and I knew he had done wrong. That is, until the truth emerged some weeks later that every rumor had been 100 percent untrue. He was not, nor had he ever been, a homosexual.

Those are the painful lessons that have come from my own lack of integrity.

LAME FRIENDSHIP

I shared the following experience about a friendship that stumbled in my book, *The Fine Art of Friendship*. It concerns Bob Pierce, the founder of World Vision.

I first met Bob at a Youth For Christ Conference in Medicine Lake, Minnesota, at the second annual conference of YFC. I took to him immediately, and we began what would become a long friendship. I was next with him at the great World Congress on Evangelism in Beatenberg, Switzerland, in 1948. During that time he was carrying on his significant missionary activities and evangelism in China. It was also the time when he wrote in his Bible, "Let my heart be broken with the things that break the heart of God," which became his life's slogan.

Bob and Dr. Frank C. Phillips then organized World Vision officially as an incorporated body in 1950. During those early years I was very close to Bob Pierce. I was a frequent guest in his home, and I often spoke on his Mutual Network radio broadcast in California. Bob also came to our home in Wheaton, Illinois, on numerous occasions. We would talk, pray, laugh, and enjoy each other to the point where our friendship fast became one of supreme importance to both of us.

In 1963 when I resigned as president of Youth For Christ International, Bob invited me to meet with the World Vision Board of Directors. I was invited to become executive vice-president of World Vision. Bob said the Lord had laid my name on his heart, and he asked me if I would be willing to consider coming with him in this new role. I told him I wasn't sure, but I would certainly pray about it. After meeting twice with the World Vision board, I accepted their invitation to become the executive vice-president.

It was September 1963. When I came with World Vision, I knew there were obstacles and challenges to Bob Pierce's vision, but I was unaware just how great some of those obstacles were. I soon learned World Vision was in deep financial trouble. We had over $440,000 in debts hanging over our heads from the great Tokyo Crusade Bob had directed. We were also falling behind about $30,000 each month with Bob's radio broadcasts (which was a lot of money in those days—and still is!).

I revealed these realities to the board at a special meeting in Laguna Beach, California, in the fall of 1963. Bob was smitten, literally upended at my report. He asked for a leave of absence, which was granted by the board. For the next year, I was instructed to do all I could to bring some order out of what I sensed was absolute chaos.

"A ROOT OF BITTERNESS"

Bob never forgave me for what he said was my "stealing" of his organization and for "taking him off the air." There were tremendous tensions, angry words, and unpleasant encounters for that entire one year—tensions that continued when Bob returned for his final two years as president of World Vision.

Later, Bob Pierce resigned, but he did so with what he said was "bitterness in his heart." He continued to hold me responsible for his leaving. Our friendship seemed to be on its last legs. That was in 1968.

In 1973, I was in Africa conducting World Vision business when I received a cable from Bob. He referred to his "root of bitterness" in the cable. He asked if we could meet together upon my return home. I cabled him immediately and said I would call him the hour I returned to Los Angeles, which I did.

The next day, Bob and I met at noon at the Derby Restaurant near the World Vision offices. We parted at five o'clock. We looked each other in the eye as we shared our hurts and fears, wept, and listened to each other as we had never listened before. We prayed until we could pray no more, listened until we could listen no more, with the one theme of our prayer being that our hearts would be reunited. It was the most exhausting personal encounter I've ever known, but during those five hours Bob and I began to understand many of the problems basic to our separation.

I had thought, when I came to California, that I was coming as Bob Pierce's friend. He saw me coming as his employee and the person to assist him in running the organization. When we really started listening to each other, we discovered each of us had an entirely different concept of what my role was to be.

As we sat across from each other for those five hours in that restaurant, we finally cleared the air. This paved the way for our reconciliation. Although our friendship was never again blessed with the openness and beauty of those earlier years, we had done what was necessary to restore the relationship. From that day forward, Bob and I were able to be comfortable with each other right up to the day he went to be with the Lord.

LET THE GUILTY GO FREE

It's hard to admit a mistake. But I'm not the only one with this problem.

Once when Frederick II, an eighteenth-century king of Prussia, went on an inspection tour of a Berlin prison, he was greeted with the cries of prisoners, who fell on their knees and protested their unjust imprisonment. While listening to these pleas of innocence, Frederick's eye was caught by a solitary figure in the corner, a prisoner seemingly unconcerned with all the commotion.

"Why are you here?" Frederick asked him.

"Armed robbery, Your Majesty."

"Were you guilty?" the king asked.

"Oh yes, indeed, Your Majesty. I entirely deserve my punishment." At that Frederick summoned the jailer. "Release this guilty man at once," he said. "I will not have him kept in this prison where he will corrupt all the fine innocent people who occupy it."[2]

Both the king and the convicts were looking at the same group of men. But the prisoners saw the heads of gold and the king had cast his gaze on the feet of broken clay.

"Blessed Are the Feet"

God's Word places tremendous importance on our feet. "How beautiful upon the mountains are the feet of him who brings good news" (Isa. 52:7). Christ washed the feet of His disciples and admonished us through the apostle Paul to have our feet shod "with the preparation of the gospel of peace" (Gal. 6:15). From the Book of Revelation we discover that Christ in His glorified form today has "feet like fine brass, refined in a furnace" (Rev. 1:17). And we know that one of the places in which they were refined was the fiery furnace of Nebuchadnezzar. "I see four men loose, *walking in the midst of the fire,* and they are not hurt, and the form of the fourth is like the Son of God" (Dan. 3:25, italics mine).

It seems abundantly clear. God is concerned about us and our integrity from head to toe.

Let's now summarize what we've learned in this chapter by means of:

INTEGRITY ACTION PLAN #6

1. Lean on the Lord as you stand on your own two feet.
2. Recognize that others will stumble, but brace yourself to help them.
3. Protect your feet of clay by "having shod your feet with the preparation of the gospel of peace" (Gal. 6:15).

We've concentrated more on the feet of clay in this chapter. But as we step out into the new millennium of the twenty-first century, it becomes increasingly obvious that God wants us to aspire for the head of gold as well.

7

~ ――――――――――――――――― ~

New Rules for a
New Millennium

This book will be "old" by the year 2000. But I'm confident its contents will stand the test of time. Without the principles of integrity we've been discussing here, there might not be any libraries or readers on that historic date.

> "There is no limit to the height a man can
> attain by remaining on the level."
>
> *Jacob M. Braude*

Chapter 6 presented the dangers of trying to walk the paths of life on fragile feet of clay. Now we'll discover how much more difficult that becomes when you reach the end of the path and start blazing new trails over stones and through the brush. The need for developing a head of gold and feet to match becomes even more urgent as we march out of the twentieth century and into the uncharted wilds of the new millennium beyond.

OVER TWENTY-ONE

In a matter of a few short years, society will enter the twenty-first century. This age is fraught with a hundred times more apprehension than what a parent encounters when an adolescent turns twenty-one. Familiar problems multiply and new fears emerge—each with perplexing questions of integrity.

Besides the obvious issues of nuclear survival, population control, and food production, look at some of the labyrinthine questions we will face as we move into the next century:

—Test-tube babies: Who qualifies for the service? Which egg lives? What do you do with the left-over fertilized eggs that don't get implanted?

—Biotech engineering: Who owns the life forms created? Who pays for the mistakes? Who protects the environment from hostile microbes?

—Nuclear power: How do we take advantage of the benefits of this resource while protecting society from accidents and lethal waste?

—Toxic waste: How do we keep advancing our high tech society without burying ourselves in poisonous trash?

—Arms race: How does one nation protect itself against nuclear weapons, particle beams, toxins, and other exotic threats without increasing the possibility that these weapons will actually be used?

—Space exploration: How do we keep advancing the new frontiers in space at an acceptable cost in terms of human life and GNP? How do we protect space from militarization?

—Medical advances: Now that we can perform operations before birth and forestall the aging process through organ transplants and replacement, how do we control the cost and distribution of these miracles? In one hospital room you find a nurse disposing of fetal remains from an abortion, while in the next room doctors are racing to save a "premature baby" only a few days older. In one room technicians preserve the life of a comatose patient through external life support systems while in the next room interns are "dumping" an indigent accident victim on another hospital because of a lack of insurance coverage. Who will arbitrate these issues of life and death?

—Urbanization: With people flocking to the cities for

jobs and survival (Mexico City is expected to be the world's largest city with 32 million inhabitants by 2000), how can we cope with crowding, crime, and overpopulation, plus the resultant loss of crop lands and forests (which produce the oxygen and food to support these millions)?

When you consider other trends such as pornography, drugs, AIDS, crime, and so on, you begin to feel the sharklike teeth on the dilemmas we face in the twenty-first century. If we're having trouble understanding and following the laws of integrity today—during an age we feel we comprehend—how are we going to manage the affairs of an even braver new world we don't understand?

NEW RULES

Remember the book *1984* by George Orwell? When it was written in 1948 its prophetic look at society seemed so new and advanced. But 1984 has now come and gone. Orwell's prophecy has "failed." However, for nearly forty years this fiction has stirred real feelings in the hearts of millions. Feelings which live on today.

The truth of the book you are now reading will be "new" for less than twenty years (when A.D. 2000 arrives). But its truth will never grow old. "If it's true, it's not new," is an adage I learned from Rick Warren of Saddleback Valley Community Church. (He's busy turning California Yuppies into Yummies, Young Urban Missionaries.) Solomon tells us there's "nothing new under the sun." But my responsibility is to take the timeless commands of God and apply them to the temporary lives of mortals.

During the last few hours of His life, Jesus felt compelled to give His disciples a "new" commandment. They already had the Ten Commandments from Moses, and Christ had long since enlarged the meaning of these to include the spirit as well as the law. Now He was delivering two other "great commandments" upon which the Law and the Prophets would hang. But still He wanted to leave them with a "new" commandment as a legacy before His death and burial.

He stated it simply, "A new commandment I give to you, that you love one another *as I have loved you*" (John 13:34). It was new because the world was yet to experience the full extent of how much "I have loved you"—to the point of unjust execution. That new commandment imparted a new dimension to the disciples' love for one another—and the power of that "new" law is just as alive for you and me these two millennia later.

The rules I will cover in this chapter are actually not new at all. Sages have recited them for centuries. But just as Christ's commandment was filled with a new dimension, so these rules—which are really reminders—are filled with a new dynamic because of our historic age.

What is that new dimension? We can better understand after we discuss these "new" rules for the new millennium.

RULE #1: GIVE OF YOUR BEST IN THE WORST OF TIMES

How bad are the times in which we live?

If the previous chapters haven't already answered that question, here's another log on the fire from a noted authority.

"A moral and ethical crisis of the first dimension" is gripping the United States, according to pollster George M. Gallup, Jr.

"The crisis is so deep that even church attendance makes little difference in a person's ethical views and behavior," Gallup told the twenty-sixth annual Minnesota Prayer Breakfast.[1]

He cited widespread cheating on taxes, an "epidemic" of extramarital affairs, and massive defaults on federal education loans as examples of our increasing moral decline.

Take a look at your daily newspaper! As I read mine recently, I was reminded that California is caught in the grip of freeway insanity. Over the past several weeks forty motorists have been shot at by fellow drivers or snipers. The madness seems to feed on itself. To date four people have died, and fifteen have been wounded. And by the time this book is in your hands, there's no telling how many more victims will be added to this growing list. Even a small aircraft pilot was threatened at gunpoint by another pilot.

Ironically, the result of this freeway madness has been better road courtesy and an increase in defensive driving. I signal and the other drivers let me change lanes. I speed up and they move over. Not out of integrity, but out of *fear*. It's a sad commentary on the times when an entire population improves its character at the point of a gun!

And just yesterday, an even more violent manifestation of this dementia stopped every heart on the street where I work. Only a matter of blocks from the World Vision headquarters here in the quiet suburban streets of Monrovia, California, an irate boyfriend ran his lover's car off the road and killed her with two blasts from a shotgun. Hours later he took his own life with the same weapon when authorities surrounded his home. I've traveled to some of the most dangerous areas of our world and have skirted terrorist-held enclaves with less feelings of threat. I thought I'd seen it all *over there*. Now I'm seeing it in spades *right here*.

Well has The Prophet spoken through Paul's epistle, "But know this, that in the last days *perilous times* will come" (2 Tim. 3:1).

How do we survive? How do we cope? Who has the answers? In times such as these, our best defense is . . .

FRIENDS—WHO KEEP US HONEST

One of my close friends, Russ Reid, and I were having lunch the other day. Russ is a long-time business associate, one whom I encouraged during the birth of his advertising agency. In the years since, he has helped us significantly at World Vision in our mission to reach people throughout the world for Christ.

As we talked, the subject quickly turned to integrity. After all I was writing a book on the subject and needed as much input from my friends as I could get. Russ reminded me that within the broad category of integrity, the "sub-category" of *accountability* was perhaps the greatest prize of all. He reflected that when Christian leaders, pastors, educators, homemakers, and others, hold their power loosely and listen to the counsel of others, they become more open and accountable. However, when they become tight-fisted with their thinking, and when they choose to "go it alone" the results are usually devastating. We need each other. There simply must be others with whom we consciously share our most intimate thoughts.

Russ's words set the tone for our lunch as we opened up to each other even more—taking the risk of choosing to be vulnerable. We talked about the need for accountability with our families, friends, and fellow workers. We further agreed that accountability starts with *yours truly*—with an honest appraisal of who we are, of what makes us tick. This includes a long, hard look at our own ideals and motives. The process must begin with a "self-inspection" tour. After all, if you and I are not honest with ourselves, how will we ever be authentic to others? However, when you and I give an accurate account of what we think and what we do, then those around us can come to rely on us with confidence.

Another colleague and close friend, Dr. James Dobson, founder of Focus on the Family, stresses the importance of getting together to review plans and review actions. "Men need to turn off the television and get together on a regular basis to ask themselves, 'How can I be a better husband, father, and worker?' Women need to sit down and discuss how they can help each other meet the needs of family and friends."[2]

We need help from each other. About the only thing we can do well by ourselves is fail.

The need for such accountability through our friendships is even greater for those in leadership positions.

Bill Hybels, pastor of the Willow Creek Community Church in South Barrington, Illinois, says, "I walk with a group of three brothers. I share much of my own personal life and they are free to correct me. In fact they delight in correcting me. This keeps me accountable."[3]

THE 2/4/6 CLUB

Many years ago I heard another friend of mine, Pastor Ray Stedman, talk about a special group of men he had gathered to meet with him on a weekly basis. These men were not all members of his congregation, but were close friends who held each other accountable in their spiritual walk. He said his experience with that small group was one of the most meaningful in his life.

After thinking about it, and realizing the need for

such accountability in my own life, I talked to my pastor about it. Dr. Ray Ortlund was interested. He expressed similar deep needs and feelings, so we met a couple of times to discuss the concept. Then we invited several men to meet with us. Some of the original group dropped out, but ultimately there were six of us who met together periodically for more than ten years in a local restaurant. We called it the 2/4/6 Club, indicating that there were six of us, who met on the second and fourth Friday mornings of each month for breakfast. We met at 7:00 A.M. for approximately an hour and a half.

It was not a prayer group—although we did pray together. It was not a Bible study group—although we did spend time in the Word. It was a time of meeting and growing together, appreciating each other and sharing our individual spiritual pilgrimages. There was no appointed leader and no agenda. We met to share experiences, to laugh and to weep. We rejoiced in our successes. We also shared and were open about our failures.

Those meetings have literally changed my life.

ECFA—The Other Half of Stewardship

This need for accountability goes beyond our friends and personal lives.

In Chapter 2, I spoke of abuses which sometimes take place when Christian organizations fail to make proper disclosure of their incomes. Headlines and weekly news magazine covers are still filled with such revelations. I promised a closer look at the workings of an organization that protects the Christian donor.

I had the privilege, along with George Wilson of the Billy Graham Association, of co-founding the Evangelical Council for Financial Accountability in 1979 to protect donors from unscrupulous practices. "Part of the problem is that we've only been taught half of stewardship," said Arthur Borden, present president of the ECFA. "We've been taught how to give but not where to give, what to expect from the organization we're supporting."[4]

Before being accepted into the Evangelical Council for Financial Accountability, potential members must show they meet some tough criteria. (I include the list here for the benefit of all who choose to be accountable.)

1. *Truthfulness in communication:* All representations of fact, description of financial condition of the organization, or narrative about events must be current, complete, and accurate. References to past activities or events must be appropriately dated. There must be no material omissions or exaggerations of fact or use of misleading photographs or any other communication that would tend to create a false impression or misunderstanding.

2. *Communication and donor expectations:* Fund-raising appeals must not create unrealistic donor expectations of what a donor's gift will actually accomplish within the limits of the organization's ministry.

3. *Communication and donor intent:* All statements made by the organization in its fund-raising appeals about the use of the gift must be honored by the organization. The donor's intent is related to both what was communicated in the appeal and to any donor instructions accompanying the gift. The organization should be aware that communications made in fund-raising appeals may indeed create a legally binding restriction.

4. *Projects unrelated to a ministry's primary purpose:* An organization raising or receiving funds for programs that are not part of its present or prospective ministry, but are proper in accordance with its exempt purpose, must either treat them as restricted funds and

channel them through an organization that can carry out the donor's intent, or return the funds to the donor.

5. *Incentives and premiums:* Fund-raising appeals which, in exchange for a contribution, offer premiums or incentives (the value of which is not insubstantial, but which is significant in relation to the amount of the donation) must advise the donor of the fair market value of the premium or incentive and that the value is not deductible for tax purposes.

6. *Reporting:* An organization must provide, on request, a report, including financial information, on the project for which it is soliciting gifts.

7. *Percentage compensation for fund-raisers:* Compensation of outside fund-raising consultants based directly or indirectly on a percentage of what is raised, or on any other contingency agreement, may create potential conflicts and opportunities for abuse. Full disclosure of such arrangements is required, at least annually, in the organization's audited financial statements, in which the disclosure must match income and related expenses. Compensation to the organization's own employees on a percentage or contingency basis is not allowed.

8. *Tax-deductible gifts for a named recipient's personal benefit:* Tax-deductible gifts may not be used to pass money or benefits to any named individual for personal use.

9. *Conflict of interest on royalties:* An officer, director, or other principal of the organization must not receive royalties for any product that is used for fund-raising or promotional purposes by his/her own organization.

10. *Acknowledgment of gifts in kind:* Property or gifts in kind received by an organization should be acknowledged, describing the property or gift accurately

without a statement of the gift's market value. It is the responsibility of the donor to determine the fair market value of the property for tax purposes. But the organization should inform the donor of IRS reporting requirements for all gifts in excess of $5,000.

11. *Acting in the interest of the donor:* An organization must make every effort to avoid accepting a gift from or entering into a contract with a prospective donor that would knowingly place a hardship on the donor, or place the donor's future well-being in jeopardy.

12. *Financial advice:* The representative of the organization, when dealing with persons regarding commitments on major estate assets, must seek to guide and advise donors so they have adequately considered the broad interests of the family and the various ministries they are currently supporting before they make a final decision. Donors should be encouraged to use the services of their attorneys, accountants, or other professional advisers.[5]

How badly are these integrity "rules" needed today? A recent telephone poll conducted by Media General-Associated Press of 1,348 adult Americans revealed the following: Slightly more than half—53 percent—said they didn't believe money collected by television evangelists generally went to good causes. *Only 27 percent* believed the money was used for good purposes.[6]

Tough standards are desperately needed today. Will it be any different in the twenty-first century? For more information about the reputable organizations that have joined the ECFA, I encourage you to write for a complete listing of all 400 (plus) members. The address for the Evangelical Council for Financial Accountability is P.O. Box 17511, Washington, D.C. 20041.

AND THE INSIDE TOO

Giving of our best in the worst of times means being wholehearted from the inside out.

Cliff Jones tells an amusing story about a close friend in Boston: "This man is intellectual, capable, and before he retired, he was the head of a prominent company. Some years ago he was bothered by a toothache. This puzzled him because he had always brushed his teeth regularly. Upon visiting his dentist he was genuinely surprised to learn that people are supposed to brush on the inside as well as the outside of their teeth. He had been religiously cleaning only the front!"[7]

A bit hard to believe, but true. It illustrates our proclivity to clean the visible exterior and to assume the inside, which we cannot see, will somehow take care of itself. Christ encountered this same phenomenon with the Pharisees. They wanted to clean the outside of the platter and leave the inside full of vile and disgusting motives (Matt. 23:25).

We can overcome this attitude as long as we remain aware and vigilant.

RULE #2: LOOK UP TO THOSE BENEATH YOU

One of the major undercurrents eroding integrity is pride. It's "common thinking" to look down on those beneath us. Yet the wisdom of both man and God is filled with admonitions about esteeming others better than self. But how can we do this if we feel we really *are* better than another? Such is the case with parent over child, veteran over newcomer, boss over employee. How does a "superior" person build integrity by making others feel elevated?

COMPANY OF GIANTS

David Ogilvy, founder of the advertising giant, Ogilvy and Mather, reinforced the importance of this principle among his executives by sending a Russian doll to each person newly appointed to head an office in the Ogilvy and Mather chain.

The doll contains five progressively smaller dolls. The message inside the smallest one reads: "If each of us hires people who are smaller than we are, we shall become a company of dwarfs. But if each of us hires people who are bigger than we are, Ogilvy and Mather will become a company of giants."[8]

One way to look up to those beneath you is by giving them room to grow into giants.

IBM—CORE OF ITS BELIEF SYSTEM

One of the giants of the business world is IBM. Did it become this way by looking down on the little guy? I found an enlightening interview with a legend at IBM, F. G. (Buck) Rodgers, former vice-president of marketing, and company dynamo for thirty-five years. His observations and philosophies are worth putting into practice.[9]

Question: The IBM philosophy of business has become almost legendary. What makes it so special?

Rodgers: It is based on three beliefs: first, respect for the individual; second, to give the best service of any company in the world; and third, to expect excellence from what people do. This was the idea of Tom Watson, Sr. when he started the business back in 1914.

Question: What is the core of your belief system, if you had to sum it up in one basic principle?

Rodgers: The thing I stress all the time is that you have to do a thousand things 1 percent better, not just do one thing 1,000 percent better. It's doing the little things well, returning phone calls, saying "thank you" to people. It sounds like a simplistic cliché, but that is the reason one organization or one person is successful and another is not. The secret is that everybody knows what they ought to be doing, but the ones who practice daily excellence are the real difference makers.[10]

Much of that excellence stems from placing the needs of the customer (beneath you) *above* your own. In fact, earlier in this interview Buck Rodgers explained that a "company's organization structure should be inverted, with the customer at the top and sales reps and management underneath." Rodgers' commitment to the customer even went so far as to give priority to appointments with customers when they conflicted with meetings in the IBM executive suite.[11]

FIVE RULES FOR DEALING WITH OTHERS

A research organization polled 500 executives, asking them what traits they thought were most important in dealing with others. From the information received, five basic "rules" were formulated. I like them because each one helps enlarge the other person. They are:

1. Always give your people the credit that is rightfully theirs. To do otherwise is both morally and ethically dishonest.

2. Be courteous. Have genuine consideration for other people's feelings, wishes, and situations.

3. Never tamper with the truth. Never *rationalize*. What you might *like* to believe is not necessarily the truth.

4. Be concise in your writing and talking, especially when giving instructions to others.

5. Be generous. Remember that it is the productivity of *others* that makes possible your executive position.[12]

People have greater motivation to understand and apply these principles in business—where the dollars count. But these concepts are equally important among family and friends. Families such as yours and mine are in dire need of help from above. It could easily start with big sister, Mom, or Dad. (That's you and me.) Looking up to those beneath you is one of the stepping stones of integrity.

RULE #3: STAND UP FOR YOUR CONVICTIONS

Those beneath us are but part of our world. Another strata exists over our heads. These include parents, older brothers and sisters, the boss (or bosses), police, city hall, the IRS, your pastor, to name but a few. And sometimes it feels as if all of these are looking over our shoulders and breathing down our necks.

When I say "stand up" to these superiors, I'm not talking about insubordination, hostility, or rebellion. I'm talking about esteem and conviction.

Some people may look down on you because they have personal problems dealing with their own authority. Others may look down on you because they care about you and want to help you become larger than they are (like the Russian doll). In either case, our reaction must be the same. We should stand up for what we believe. That way if we're right we'll gain ground. If we're wrong, we'll find out sooner.

This story by Nido Qubein illustrates my point.

An Eastern bishop was accustomed to paying an annual visit to a small religious college. On one such visit, the bishop engaged in an after-dinner conversation with the college president. The religious leader offered the opinion that the millennium could not be long in coming since everything about nature had been discovered, and all possible inventions had been made. The college president disagreed, stating that he felt the next fifty years would bring amazing discoveries and inventions. In his opinion, human beings would be flying through the skies like the birds within a relatively short time.

"Nonsense!" shouted the bishop. "Flight is reserved for the angels!"

The bishop's name was Wright. He had two sons—Orville and Wilbur.[13]

Fortunately for American aviation, the bishop's two sons were willing to join the college president in "standing up" for their beliefs and convictions.

As important as holding ground when you're right is the willingness to give ground when you're wrong. The challenge we all face is knowing which attitude is appropriate.

Fortunately, we're not left to our own guesswork. In matters of conviction and integrity, we have ample direction—as this remark from Abraham Lincoln demonstrates: "All the good from the Savior of the world is communicated through this Book; but for the Book we could not know right from wrong. All the things desirable to man are contained in it."

I've wrestled often with questions of integrity. Here are some passages from "the Book" that helped me keep my eye on the north star of conscience:

By pride comes only contention, but with the well advised is wisdom (Prov. 13:10).

The law of the wise is a fountain of life, to turn away from the snares of death (Prov. 13:14).

Poverty and shame will come to him who disdains correction, but he who regards reproof will be honored (Prov. 13:18).

He who walks with wise men will be wise, but the companion of fools will be destroyed (Prov. 13:20).

Faithful are the wounds of a friend, but the kisses of an enemy are deceitful (Prov. 27:6).

There are dozens of other passages that will help you decide when to dig in your heels or when to hang up your boots. In fact I agree with President Lincoln in recommending that you read the entire Book. But these passages have been useful to me in sorting out these matters of integrity. I'm confident they can benefit you as well.

Dr. E. M. Griffin gave an interesting comment when addressing a writer's conference at Wheaton College several years ago. It purportedly came from Ted Kennedy's speech writer. "Those are my views. If you don't like them, let me know and I'll change them."

That's the exact antithesis of everything I want to convey in this chapter. It tells you what will *not* work as a new rule for the new millennium ahead. But let's take a brief look once again at what *will work* for you and for me.

INTEGRITY ACTION PLAN #7

1. Give of your best in the worst of times.
2. Look up to those beneath you.
3. Stand up for your convictions.

These are my new—and yet ancient—rules for the new millennium. Earlier I alluded to the "new commandment" from Jesus. "A new commandment I give to you, that you love one another *as I have loved you.*" It was new because of His profoundly new example of *how* to reach out to one another.

What imparts newness to these rules we have been discussing? My answer is this. We must love integrity *as the world has loved iniquity.* These are perilous times. Iniquity could bring near global extinction through all-out war (intentional or accidental), viral infection, ozone depletion, nuclear power accident, bio-misengineering, to name but a few. But even as the Marines look for a few good men, let's you and I be men and women with the kind of integrity that reverses these terrible trends.

I said earlier that this book will be "old" by the year 2000. But I'm confident its contents will stand the test of time. Without the principles of integrity we've been discussing here, there might not be any libraries or readers on that historic date.

These rules are new because the challenges of the twenty-first century are new. My prayer is that you will take these principles to heart and put them to use. The workers of iniquity are gaining momentum. So must the workers of integrity.

Join me now in Chapter 8 for a look at the road map ahead.

8

The High Road
to Integrity

Though she was a prostitute, I doubt that this woman was a total stranger to the high road of integrity. Along with the muddy clay of her character, she displayed a remarkable iron will.

> "Talent is nurtured in solitude; character is formed in the stormy billows of the world."
>
> *Johann Wolfgang von Geothe*

Southern California is well endowed with mountains. There's Mount Baldy and San Jacinto, both towering over 10,000 feet. The San Gabriel mountains rise 8,000 feet just a few short miles from my own backyard. Farther north, you'll find the rugged Sierras and Mount Shasta, well over 14,000 feet. Over the years my family and I have enjoyed an occasional escape to these heavenly retreats as a respite from the pressures of work. So when it comes to mountains, I feel I've learned a few things about the "high road."

Mountain roads are much like corkscrews to the sky. From the bottom, you see them winding up to the clouds and wonder, "How can we ever get up there?" Along the way you've got to concentrate on the road ahead and forget about the unseen dangers around the next corner or off the sheer ledge to one side. But as the sky above and the panorama beneath race each other to the horizon, you begin to catch glimpses of the road below. If you're like me, sometimes you find yourself wondering, "Were we ever really down there?"

The path to integrity is like a mountain road with all its challenges and rewards. In this chapter, we'll meet some people who turned off the road and lost their way. But we'll see how they came back to mark the trail, making it easier for you and me to stay on the mountain pathway to success and happiness we call integrity.

"When Do We Get the Girls?"

If someone else is sliding off into the ravine below, that's no excuse for you and me to join them. You'll see what I mean in this story told by Cliff Jones in his book, *Winning through Integrity:*

I had not been married very long when the head of our firm called me to his office. He told me that a most important client from a distant city would be in town that night. It seemed that none of our senior executives was available to have dinner with this man who controlled a large account. So he assigned me to the task.

Right after work, I proudly picked this man up at his hotel and took him to one of the city's best restaurants. We passed a delightful couple of hours, and I was congratulating myself on doing a great job for the firm when without warning, he asked a blunt question that caused my bubble to collapse. As he lit up an after-dinner cigar, he looked hard at me and said, "When do we get the girls?"

For a moment I was speechless as I tried to think fast. This was totally unexpected, and I decided to be candid about that. I told him that the thought had not entered my mind. I confessed that I had not the foggiest notion of where to obtain a call girl or prostitute for him. But realizing that my response could lose this account, I came up with what turned out to be a darn good solution.

During dinner he had mentioned that he liked to sing. Luckily, I had remembered that. Quickly I said, "Mr.

Blank, you said you liked to sing. Well, I have a little bride at home who is a musician. She can play the piano by ear so well I'll bet you can't think of a song she can't play."

"Let's go see," he said and off we went.

I alerted my wife, and when we arrived there was more food and drink awaiting us. She played, and we three sang for what seemed like hours. He had a rotten voice, but he thoroughly enjoyed himself. So much so, in fact, that on future trips to our city, he never again mentioned girls but only coming to my house to sing.[1]

THE LOW ROAD

We learn a great deal about the high road of integrity by looking down on the low road of compromise. Focusing on the down side of the issue, a team of psychologists at the University of California wondered what sort of people *lacked* the integrity to be good leaders. Here are some of the characteristics they discovered:

Aggressive against people who do not agree with them, or who do not do as they want them to.

Apprehensive that others are scheming against them, or the firm.

Fatalistic in thinking that most workers aren't to be trusted; intolerant of democratic leaders.

Inflexible, believing that there must be no deviation from the course they have set.

Impulsive, preferring action to thinking it over before acting.

Prejudiced against certain social groups, firms, religions, or nations.

Submissive in blindly believing in, and following, forceful leaders or achievers whom they admire.[2]

Seeing people lose the path through detours such as these reminds me of a remark by the great statesman and Civil War orator, Edward Everett. "Though a hundred crooked paths may conduct to a temporary success, the one plain and straight path of public and private virtue can alone lead to a pure and lasting fame and the blessings of posterity."

IF YOU HAVE STUMBLED

None of us lives a perfect life. We all stumble. Just as I owned up to some of my shortcomings in Chapter 6, so all of my readers have made mistakes. But sometimes we compound that error by making the additional mistake of thinking, "There's no hope. I've gone too far." Yes, the Word of God does allude to an "unpardonable sin" in Matthew 12:31–32. But the only factor that makes it unpardonable is the refusal by an unrepentant sinner to *ask* for pardon. Anyone who confesses a mistake and asks for forgiveness will be forgiven. "If we confess our sins, He is faithful and just to forgive us our sins and to cleanse us from all unrighteousness" (1 John 1:9).

You and I don't have to settle for failure. We can pick ourselves up and continue the journey no matter how badly we may have fallen. All it takes is confidence and courage. That's why the Bible has preserved so many uplifting examples for us.

FAVOR, FAILURE, FAVOR

Samson was born with a special favor from God. As long as he honored the command to let his hair grow long and refrain from wine, he would possess the strength of an army. In fact, God intended to use Samson for delivering the Israelites from their Philistine oppressors (Judg. 13:5). So great was his power that Samson discovered he could withstand entire legions of men singlehandedly. In one decisive battle, he took up the jawbone of an ass and slew 1,000 Philistines. This eased the burden of Israel's oppression enough for Samson to stumble.

Iron men often make heavy mistakes. Though none of the opposing warriors could defeat him in battle, one of their delicate maidens was able to overthrow him by seducing his integrity. "Now afterward it happened that he loved a woman in the Valley of Sorek whose name was Delilah. And the lords of the Philistines came up to her and said to her, 'Entice him, and find out where his great strength lies, and by what means we may overpower him'" (Judg. 16:5).

Where chains, swords, and spears had been futile in bringing Samson to his knees, beguiling words did the deed. After some difficulty Delilah discovered "all his heart" about the secret power of his vow to God. "If I am shaven, then my strength will leave me, and I shall become weak, and be like any other man" (v. 17).

If falling for a Gentile woman didn't warn him about a breach of integrity; if consorting with the enemy didn't cause him to worry; if breaking the commandment against adultery didn't stir his fear, then I begin to understand how Samson actually allowed Delilah to lull him to sleep on her lap and call for a man to shave the seven locks from his head.

The spiritual blindness which led Samson over the edge and off the high road to integrity also exacted a painful physical price. "Then the Philistines took him and put out his eyes, and brought him down to Gaza. They bound him with bronze fetters, and he became a grinder in the prison" (v. 21).

The enemy had conquered the great Samson, leaving him alone with his sorrow.

But godly sorrow is often enough. Soon his hair began to grow back again, and with it came a brighter vision of his mission for God—a vision that penetrated his darkened eyes, sparked his spirit, and renewed his former great strength. From this failure, Samson was able to regain favor with his God.

Smug and complacent, the gloating Philistines called a huge assembly on behalf of their pagan deity. Some three thousand men, women, lords, and ladies gathered to worship and taunt Samson. The two forces were pitted against each other. While the Philistines prayed to Dagon, Samson prayed to the God who would be his deliverance. "Strengthen me, I pray, just this once, O God, that I may with one blow take vengeance on the Philistines for my two eyes!" (Judg. 16:28).

A merciful God honored Samson's return to integrity as ". . . Samson took hold of the two middle pillars which supported the temple, and he braced himself against them, one on his right and the other on his left. Then Samson said, 'Let me die with the Philistines!' And he pushed with all his might, and the temple fell on the lords and all the people who were in it. So the dead that he killed at his death were more than he had killed in his life" (v. 29–30).

I find myself wondering what God's answer might have been had Samson altered his final prayer to ask, "Let me live to celebrate this destruction of the Philistines." Nonetheless, God gave him the victory because he returned to the high road of integrity.

A FORMER HARLOT

Another lost "Christian" who later found her way was Rahab. I put Christian in quotes because she lived before the time of Christ. But Paul tells us that Moses (who also lived B.C.) esteemed "the reproach of *Christ* greater riches than the treasures in Egypt" (Heb. 11:26). So I feel justified in calling this fellow member of the faith chapter a Christian.

Though she was a prostitute, I doubt that this woman was a total stranger to the high road of integrity. Along with the muddy clay of her character, she displayed a remarkable iron will.

When two foreign lookouts from Israel sought safe-haven in Jericho, Rahab took them in. Not because she needed another trick to pay the rent, but because, "I know that the Lord has given you the land" (Josh. 2:9).

How did she know the God of righteousness was replacing the sinful inhabitants of the land with a new group of people who had promised to keep His holy laws? Maybe her understanding wasn't that complete, but she did realize "the Lord your God, He is God in heaven above and on earth beneath" (v. 12).

I've worked with people long enough to realize that anyone willing to profess Christ and risk his or her life on His behalf is on the road to repentance and conversion. There can be little doubt that Rahab wanted to change her present life and focus on the needs of others. "Now, therefore, I beg you, swear to me by the Lord, since I have shown you kindness, that you also will show kindness to my father's house, and give me a true token, and spare my father, my mother, my brothers, my sisters, and all that they have, and deliver our lives from death" (v. 12–13).

It's interesting to note that before she ever received a promise of protection, Rahab had *already* risked her life by hiding the spies from the guards at Jericho (v. 6). Notice her faith. She believed in the God of Israel. She believed the Israelites would conquer her hometown. She believed the Israelite spies would keep their promise. And she believed this boldly enough to convince "her father's household and all that she had" that they should not fight for Jericho, but wait in her home for deliverance at the hands of the invaders (Josh. 6:25).

Her heroic actions caught the attention of no less than three authors of the Bible. The writer to the Hebrews tells us in his "faith chapter," "by faith the harlot Rahab did not perish with those who did not believe" (11:31). James writes, "Was not Rahab the harlot also justified by works when she received the messengers and sent them out another way?" (2:25).

The third Bible author I cite gives Rahab even higher marks. In the Gospel according to Matthew, forty-two generations are reckoned in the chronology of Christ from Abraham to the Savior. Only five women are mentioned and one of them is Rahab. *Halley's Bible Handbook* tells us, "Rahab married an Israelite named Salmon (Matt. 1:5). Caleb had a son named Salmon (1 Chron. 2:51). It may have been the same Salmon. If so, then she married into a leading family of Israel, thus, becoming ancestress of Boaz, David and of Christ."[3]

Can there be any doubt that this woman who once ignored the high road of integrity found the courage to change direction for good? That opportunity is always open to you and to me.

Rahab and Samson help us find our way back onto the straight and narrow path whenever we wander. Other heroes from the Bible show us how to win the uphill battles against despair, heartbreak, and hardship and remain on the high road of integrity.

WHEREVER YOU GO, I WILL GO

Setbacks are seldom easy to accept. They reveal what we're made of inside.

Joblessness and economic depression became so bad
during the time of the Judges that a man named Elimelech
was forced to leave his native country of Bethlehem Judah
to provide for his wife, Naomi, and their two sons. They
journeyed into Moab.

As if being uprooted from her homeland wasn't
enough, Naomi soon faced another staggering setback.
Elimelech died. Impoverished and grief-stricken, she was
left with two strapping boys to guide into manhood.

As young men will do, Mahlon and Chilion soon fell in
love with two local girls. Now Orpah and Ruth became
part of Naomi's recovering life. Things seemed to be on the
upswing—two strong providers for the family and two
lovely daughters sharing their hopes for children and a
bright future.

As young men are not supposed to do, Mahlon and
Chilion also died prematurely—cut off in the prime of
their lives.

In a matter of just a few short years, Naomi lost her
native homeland, her husband, and her two sons. What
remained to help her piece together a new life?

Orpah and Ruth were wonderful young ladies. But
they were natives of Moab. Without children, what reason
would they have to stay and comfort Naomi? She of all
women understood the longings they must have felt for the
comfort of their ancestral homes and familiar surroundings.

Here was the perfect excuse for Naomi to grow bitter
toward God and selfish toward her daughters-in-law. But
how did she handle this test of integrity?

"Naomi said to her two daughters-in-law, 'Go, return
each to her mother's house. The Lord deal kindly with you,
as you have dealt with the dead and with me. The Lord
grant that you may find rest, each in the house of her
husband.' Then she kissed them, and they lifted up their
voices and wept" (Ruth 1:8–9).

What kind of character did the young ladies possess? Were they seeking their own selfish needs and interests? Or were they filled with compassion for one who shared their love for three families that were not to be?

"Surely we will return with you to your people," they offered. But again Naomi thought otherwise. "'No, my daughters; for it grieves me very much for your sakes that the hand of the Lord has gone out against me.' Then they lifted up their voices and wept again; and Orpah kissed her mother-in-law, but Ruth clung to her" (Ruth 1:13–14).

Again Naomi tried to dissuade Ruth, but to no avail. Then follows one of the most beautiful passages on loyalty and integrity in all the Bible, one which is often recited and set to beautiful music:

> Entreat me not to leave you,
> Or to turn back from following after you;
> For wherever you go, I will go;
> And wherever you lodge, I will lodge;
> Your people shall be my people,
> And your God, my God.
> Where you die, I will die,
> And there will I be buried.
> The Lord do so to me, and more also,
> If anything but death parts you and me.
> (Ruth 1:16–17)

Could anything be closer to the high road of integrity than these powerful sentiments?

The Book of Ruth then tells the story of how Ruth, with the guidance of Naomi, moved back to Bethlehem and won the heart of a prominent land holder by the name of Boaz. They married and bore a child who probably felt like he had not one, but two mothers.

The boy was Ruth's, but "the women said to Naomi,

'Blessed be the Lord, who has not left you this day without a near kinsman; and may his name be famous in Israel'" (Ruth 4:14).

He grew up with two loving women nurturing him as their own and a man of integrity as his father. (Boaz held staunchly to the statutes of Israel by allowing a "nearer kinsman" of Ruth and Naomi to exercise the right of first acceptance toward the maiden [Ruth 3:12]. Fortunately this stranger declined.) With this background, rich in integrity, the lad went on to become "famous in Israel" as the father of Jesse, thus the grandfather of David.

Like the story of Rahab, this walk on the high road still continues today. Ruth is one of the five named women who helped propagate the royal dynasty of Christ, our living High Priest.

MOVING FORWARD

Examples such as these from Ruth, Rahab, Samson, and others show us the way along this high road to integrity. But knowing the way is not always enough. We've got to keep overcoming obstacles and moving forward.

Sometimes the greatest obstacles we face are self imposed through bad habits. We can speed our progress toward integrity or any other goal by getting rid of troublesome habits. Originally I was only going to share a few of Norman Vincent Peale's thoughts on this subject. But his insights are too important to cut short. I urge you to read Dr. Peale's words carefully:

First, take responsibility for your bad habits. The Lord didn't put them into you. You put them into yourself. But He will help you get rid of them if you ask Him sincerely; you can be sure He has no use for such things.

Next, believe you can get rid of them. Not instantly, perhaps, and not all at one time. But one by one. Within a reasonable time-span. The reason most New Year's resolutions fall by the wayside is that the resolvers don't really believe that they can keep them. They don't expect to keep them. They just vaguely hope to keep them. And that's not enough.

You must begin by sending a clear, unmistakable signal to your unconscious mind. "As a man thinketh *in his heart,*" says the Bible, "so is he" (Proverbs 23:7). That word "heart," I feel sure, means the unconscious mind. To break a bad habit, then, your conscious desire to escape from it must be stronger than your unconscious wish or tendency to stay in that same old groove. If you send a halfhearted message to your unconscious mind suggesting that it might be nice to stop doing this or that, it will brush you aside and go right on its accustomed (habitual) way. No, you have to build up in your conscious mind a motivation so strong that your unconscious mind will go along with it.

Constant repetition of a specific goal or objective will eventually sink down into the unconscious mind. You can write down your habit-breaking goal on half a dozen three-by-five cards, paste one on your bathroom mirror, keep one in your pocket, have another in your desk drawer at the office, make sure one is on your bedside table where you can start the good habit of reading it last thing before you go to sleep at night. Each time you do read it, add those words: "So help me God!" Sooner or later—probably sooner—your unconscious mind is going to get the message. And when it does, when your "heart" is changed, you will change.

Another way to strengthen your motivation is to make a list of the bad habits you know you have. Then ask yourself how these traits affect other people's opinions of you. A bad habit almost always sends out a signal about the possessor of it. Usually a negative signal. Right or wrong, a nail-biter gives the impression that he is nervous and unsure of himself. The habitual name-dropper, that he has an inferiority complex. The person who is always late, that he is selfish and inconsiderate. The procrastinator, that he can't be trusted with anything that needs to be done efficiently. The user of profanity, that he has no respect for God or other people's sensibilities. Bad habits really do handicap people. That's why they're bad!

So take your list and study it carefully. Which of these disagreeable traits is doing you the most harm? Single out that one as your first target. Then go after it.

And don't visualize a struggle against tremendous odds. Visualize the victory! If you're a nail-biter, *see* yourself with attractive hands, with well-cared-for nails. If you're overweight and inactive, *see* yourself slim and energetic. Images held firmly in the mind have an almost miraculous way of becoming realities. So don't see yourself fighting to break that bad habit; see yourself triumphant because you *have* broken it![4]

Ridding ourselves of bad habits helps clear the high road for good ones.

MOUNTAIN OF THE LORD

Throughout this chapter we've looked at mountains, trails, and decisions. This "high road" of integrity demands a constant upward climb. But where does it lead? Why should we choose a high road if we don't have an equally high destination?

Interestingly enough, the biblical characters I've discussed in this chapter are referred to in Hebrews 11 as pilgrims. And where were they going? "These all died in faith, not having received the promises, but having seen them afar off were assured of them, embraced them, and confessed that they were strangers and pilgrims on the earth. For those who say such things declare plainly that they seek a homeland. But now they desire a better, that is, a heavenly country. Therefore God is not ashamed to be called their God, for He has prepared a city for them" (Heb. 11:13, 14, 16).

And where do we find that city and homeland? On the open plain or somewhere else?

"Now it shall come to pass in the latter days that the mountain of the Lord's house shall be established on the top of the mountains, and all nations shall flow to it. Many people shall come and say, 'Come, and let us go up to the mountain of the Lord, to the house of the God of Jacob'" (Isa. 2:2–3).

There's no doubt in my mind that those who rule their universe with truth, love, and compassion live on a holy mountain accessible only by taking the high road of integrity.

INTEGRITY ACTION PLAN #8

1. Look up at the goal ahead—often.
2. Glance down at the lessons below—occasionally.
3. Take heart at the success of those who have gone before.
4. Develop the good habit of breaking bad ones.

In the context of what we understand about integrity—both its absence and its abundance—Psalm 15 asks you and me a penetrating question. "Lord, who may dwell in Your holy hill?" The answer to that question is the answer to the questions being posed in the book you're holding now. Let's explore them together more fully in our final chapter.

9

A Call to Action

Strange how easy it is for little things to attract our attention and call us to action . . . Why is it that we seldom enjoy the results of "integrity living" as much as we could? Perhaps we simply don't understand the connection between right actions and right results.

> "An honest man is the noblest work of God."
> *Alexander Pope*

He looked like almost any other passenger you would see on an airplane, but I should have recognized the difference in his eyes—somehow they really cared. This was one of those long transoceanic flights that ends before it starts because you're crossing the international dateline. I've flown from Los Angeles to Tokyo more times than I care to remember, and assumed this would just be "another one of those flights": grueling, tiresome, and forgettable.

So I was somewhat relieved when this distinguished stranger took the seat next to mine. He looked like someone I could talk to—or simply pass the time in silence—depending on what the long hours invited.

"Hello, I'm Benjamin Alexander," said the stranger-no-more. "You want the window seat?" he offered.

"But you've got the boarding pass for it!" I protested mildly.

"Go ahead and take it if you'd like. I've pretty well seen it all. Besides, I enjoy the sights in here every bit as much as those outside," he said while eyeing one of the female passengers—a beguiling six- or seven-year-old with an enchanting smile.

His voice was kind. Listenable. The sort that might lull you to sleep if it didn't have something unexpected to say most of the time.

"You're Ted Engstrom, aren't you?"

"Yes, how did you know?" I said with a start.

"Well, let's just say I saw it on one of the passenger rosters."

"I didn't know they left that type of information lying around," I countered with a puzzled frown. "What line of work are you in?" From his neat appearance and smooth demeanor, I guessed sales.

"Hydro-electric power. Family business. We've been in the industry for generations."

Without giving me a chance to ask anything more, Ben pulled a newsmagazine out of his carry-on and began settling himself into the seat for taxi and take-off.

"Boong," chimed the intercom—calling us all to attention.

"Hello, and welcome to flight 712 to Tokyo," said the flight attendant stirring everyone into action extinguishing smokes, stowing handbags, and checking seatbelts.

As flight safety instructions about the Boeing 747 drifted through the cabin, my mind turned to the welter of thoughts I had been sifting through on integrity. So I couldn't help but notice that Ben was reading a recent article on broken promises in high places.

"What do you think about all these scandals?" I asked.

He lowered the magazine with a sigh and shook his head. Maybe he didn't want to discuss the issues. Or perhaps he would be filled with vituperative remarks about specific people and actions. I enjoy a stimulating conversation. But I've never felt good about gossip. These topics seem to race down the razor's edge between the two. Which side would this newcomer veer toward?

"You're a man of the Word," he said surprising me again. "What do you think about these issues?"

Rarely being at a loss for something to say, I related my disappointment and disillusionment on many of the same issues you and I have shared throughout this book. "How could responsible leaders allow themselves to fall into such irresponsible actions? How could someone expect us to honor their public decisions when their own private decisions are so dishonorable? And more pointedly, how could someone who supposedly lived by the Word of God, flagrantly disobey the instructions of the Almighty?"

I could tell Ben had something worthwhile to say, but he was cut off abruptly by the sudden wails of an infant back in the coach section. He changed his thought in midbreath.

"That child back there has much to cry about. She saw her dad for the last time yesterday and her mom is headed home to 'mom.'"

"How'd you know that?" I asked.

"Oh, just the sound of her voice I suppose—and something you said."

"Something I said?"

"Right. Another responsible leader disobeying the instructions of God."

"Huh? What leader are you talking about?"

"Her father. But don't worry, she won't cry for long. She's too young to know what's really hurting her."

This was confusing. Before I could collect my thoughts to piece together another question, the infant fell quiet and Ben handed me a knowing glance.

"Ted," he continued, "I know you've been giving these subjects a great deal of thought. Do you mind if I ask you a few questions about integrity and personal values?"

By now I was so shocked by what he was saying that nothing really surprised me anymore. "Sure, go ahead," I replied haltingly. But then I began wondering if he might know as much about a seventy-one-year-old man seated next to him as he did about a seven-month-old infant fifteen rows away. Who was this man and what was he all about?

"Excuse me, gentlemen. May I interest either of you in a cocktail?" asked the flight attendant. Her warm smile called me back into the real world at 35,000 feet in the sky.

"No, thank you," volunteered Ben. "My friend and I will have juice."

"You seem pretty confident about what I think and want."

"Maybe that's because you seem pretty confident about what you think and want. Tell me this," he continued before I could thank him for the compliment, "what difference does it make if a man drinks himself into oblivion, or sires a half-dozen children by six different women?"

"What kind of question is that?" I thought to myself.

"I'll tell you what kind of question it is, by answering it for you," Ben interrupted.

When I told you he ceased to surprise me, I was a bit premature. This remark took me completely off guard. I've been a lot of places and seen a lot of people, but *never* anything like this. In fact I began casting my eyes around the plane to make sure I wasn't in the operating room under anesthesia or something. But I was still strapped in and he wasn't about to let me go anywhere without hearing more.

"It doesn't make a bit of difference how we conduct

our lives today and tomorrow *if* we don't care about the effect these actions may have," Ben philosophized.

"OK," I said to let him know I heard, but didn't necessarily agree. He was obviously headed somewhere with this line of reasoning and I wanted to be near the mental lifeboat if it came time to jump ship.

"You see, people are very anxious to avoid actions in the future if they understand how destructive they are from direct personal experience," Ben continued. "See that elderly man across the aisle and up two seats? He would never dream of using cocaine. He's watched one grandson and a niece destroyed by the stuff. The outcome just doesn't make sense to him."

"I can understand that," I volunteered.

"But one person can never live long enough to make all the mistakes."

"Now that's something I can 'amen.' You'd have to have at least nine lives, maybe more, to do that."

"Precisely. And then we often have trouble seeing the connection between our actions and our problems. Take that businessman over there for instance—the one reaching for his cigarettes and eyeing the 'no smoking' sign. His actions and his diet are destroying his heart tissue. But he won't admit the connection in his mind till he feels the pain in his chest. And by then it may be too late."

"Well, how does all this tie in with integrity?" I asked with impatience.

"Ted, you've been around long enough to understand the problems a teen will face, and the problems of a young single man, and the problems of a newlywed couple, and the problems of young parents, and the problems of older parents, an employee, a boss . . . . "

"Yes, yes," I said cutting him off before he had me as old as Methuselah. "But how does that affect integrity?"

"Let me ask you this. Don't you think you'd have been a much better teen-age student and employee if you understood then what you understand today?"

"Obviously," I conceded.

"And a better friend, groom, father, boss—if you understood *then* what you know *today.*"

"Well, most likely," I offered. "But where are you going with all of this?"

"Have you ever tried to impart some of this understanding to others?" he continued.

I could tell he knew I'd written a number of books on many of these same subjects. "I'd want to write down these experiences and tell others about them."

"And that's exactly what we've got here," he said bending down to pull something out of his attaché case.

Maybe it's one of my books, I speculated. *He seems to know everything about me. Must have gotten that information from somewhere. But instead* . . . .

"It's all right here," he said, dropping his open palm on a Bible. "Here are the accounts of thousands of members of the same family learning about the outcomes of their decisions and passing the wisdom along to newcomers who would never live long enough to relearn everything on their own. And it's authored by someone who's been around long enough to see the outcome of each decision. That, my friend, is the source of integrity."

"Where have you been for the past 1900 years?" I asked him. (And it seemed as if this question caused him to raise one eyebrow almost imperceptibly.) "People have been preaching those words since the time of Christ and we're still making the same mistakes." His observation made a lot of sense, but I wanted to see what else he had to say.

"That's been a problem," he conceded. Then with a sigh of resignation he added, "And we've all paid dearly. That's where the second half of integrity comes into play."

"Second half? What's that?" I asked, knowing full well he was going to tell me anyway. He seemed to pause a long time in reflection. I looked at his eyes and they were moist with remembered pain.

"Someone always has to pay for the mistakes. That young couple behind us took the life of their unborn child rather than reduce their earnings to one income. The man who came onboard in the wheelchair was paralyzed when his grade school buddies dared him to dive into the creek. Without integrity, people perish."

His voice was hushed and the silence grew as loud as the nearby jet engines. About then I began to worry that he was going to say something about me and my own short-comings. So I quickly formulated another question. But he beat me to the punch.

"Ted, do you know who paid the ultimate penalty so we all wouldn't have to die for our mistakes?"

There was no doubt in my mind that he was referring to none other than our Savior, Jesus Christ.

"That's right," he responded before I could speak. And the answer seemed to mean so much more to him— almost as if he knew about the tragedy firsthand.

"Maybe if people really understood the outcome of their actions," he mused out loud, "and could see the pain it inflicts on innocent people, maybe they'd be willing to pay more attention to this matter of integrity. What do you think?"

"I think you're right."

"Then what are you going to do about it?" he slowly added to my surprise.

"Are you Mr. Ben Alexander?" the attendant leaned over and asked, startling both of us. "We have a phone call for you up front by the galley."

We both looked at each other with puzzlement and he disappeared into the galley.

That's the last time I ever saw Ben Alexander. When I became concerned about his prolonged absence, the flight attendant informed me that there was no such person on board, and the seat next to me had been vacant since we left Los Angeles. When I asked the young girl across the aisle, the retired gentleman, and the lovebirds behind me and got the same answer, I knew it was time to look somewhere else for the explanation. Not surprisingly, I spotted a small slip of paper in the vacant seat next to me with these words written on it, "Hebrews 13:2." Ninety-nine percent sure of what it said already, I hurriedly looked up the scripture. "Do not forget to entertain strangers, for by so doing some have unwittingly entertained angels."

The Message

If you asked me, "Did this really happen?" my answer might surprise you. But before I explain the mystery, there are a few more principles from Ben Alexander and from our previous chapters I want to summarize and tie together.

"What are you going to do about it?" were the parting words from the stranger I entertained. This book is much of my answer. As for me, I'm going to tell people about the importance of looking to the outcome of our actions and avoiding pain toward others.

What about you?

Strange how easy it is for little things to attract our attention and call us to action. The gentle bell aboard a jetliner directs our attention to some forthcoming message: "No smoking," or "Fasten your seatbelt." These messages touch on life and death, so we usually respond.

But look at some of the other calls that make us act—telephones, car horns, alarm clocks, elevator chimes, tea kettles, microwave oven timers, to name but a few.

We're eager and willing to be called into action when the outcome is something we enjoy. Why is it that we seldom enjoy the results of "integrity living" as much as we could? Perhaps we simply don't understand the connection between right actions and right results.

Throughout this book, we've seen a lot of people stumble. New disappointments hit the headlines every day. In fact, one of the latest letdowns involved 106 public officials in New York. After a sting operation to uncover graft, U.S. Attorney Rudolph Giuliani made the following statement, "On 106 occasions, bribes were offered or discussed. On 105 of those occasions, the public official involved accepted the bribe. And on the other occasion, he turned it down because he didn't think the amount was large enough."[1]

But is it enough to look at the shortcomings of others, wag our heads back and forth a couple of times, and assume we are protected from the same fate? I can say with assurance that the Marines who allegedly compromised the embassy in Moscow had been thoroughly warned. The TV evangelist who locked himself away in a hotel with a young church secretary had certainly preached the scriptures against adultery. The businessmen who triggered a superbowl of scandal on Wall Street thought they understood all the rules.

If we're going to put out these destructive forces in our lives, we've got to replace them with something else. It's not enough to "mistreat others as we mistreat ourselves"; we must embrace a code of ethics—that kind of "true religion" that transcends our own susceptible reasoning.

As Ben Alexander explained, it's a lot easier to control our present behavior if we deeply understand the future consequences of these actions. How could we let down our friends and family if we actually shared the pain our actions might inflict on them?

Would I betray my mate of many years if I actually felt the pain our children would suffer? Would I steal from the company supply closet if I understood the anguish some widow might experience from the higher prices resulting from my impropriety? Would I gossip about a friend if I saw my careless actions drive that person to drugs and alcohol?

These feelings and these actions make up the very heart of Christianity. The Son of God, the One who was present at the creation of the first humans, has shared His knowledge of outcomes with men and women for millennia. He then emptied Himself of divinity and became the Son of man for the express purpose of sharing and removing the pain we inflict upon ourselves. This sacrifice paves the way for our life of integrity.

I'm not asking you to become a Christian. I'm only asking you to consider how much better life might be if everyone in our world shared Christ's concern for others.

Think about it for a moment. If this were a pre-Fall Garden of Eden . . . if everyone were a true believer—an uncompromising, caring, loving, self-effacing Christian— you wouldn't have to fear for your life because there would be no hatred and murder. You wouldn't have to be concerned about the breakup of your family because your loved ones would all obey the law against adultery. You wouldn't have to endure the onslaught of sexual temptations because no one would covet your sexual favors. You wouldn't have to lock up your money because everyone would understand the outcome of stealing.

In short, you wouldn't have to fear what others might do to you. Your only fear might be what you could do to yourself.

And that brings us back full circle. Since we can't control others in this present world, the only alternative we have is to control ourselves—and that takes integrity.

THE POWER OF ONE

Never underestimate the power of one—a power that is tapped by those who gain control over themselves. One girl from Albania improved the lives of underprivileged people in thirty countries. One football player in California tackled the problems of inner city youngsters. One coach in Conyers, Georgia, inspired the whole city (and much of the nation) to "do what is honest."

Some may look at these trophy winners we showcased in Chapter 5 and throw up their hands in discouragement. Too many of us dismiss integrity as something only the superstars can achieve.

But integrity is for *everyone*. One homeowner can write an editor or lawmaker to swing an issue. One consumer can file a class action suit that will benefit millions. One bereaved mother can channel her rage into MADD (Mothers Against Drunk Driving). One teacher can provide the inspiration to motivate students for a lifetime.

ON TO THE TOP

Such commendable goals call for an extra dimension. It's been said that nothing worthwhile has ever been accomplished without enthusiasm. I certainly believe it, especially when you realize enthusiasm actually means "God in us."

We talked about the high road to integrity in Chapter 8. It leads to the "mountain of God." What better source can we go to for genuine "enthusiasm" toward integrity?

One passage that explains how to arrive at that mountain is found in the Psalms. I share it with you as one of my favorite sources of guidance.

PSALM 15

Lord, who may abide in Your tabernacle? Who may dwell in Your holy hill?

He who walks uprightly, and works righteousness, and speaks the truth in his heart;

He who does not backbite with his tongue, nor does evil to his neighbor, nor does he take up a reproach against his friend;

In whose eyes a vile person is despised. But he honors those who fear the Lord; He who swears to his own hurt and does not change;

He who does not put out his money at usury, nor does he take a bribe against the innocent.

He who does these things shall never be moved.

ACT AS IF

None of us can live in perfection all of the time. The thought of never offending someone with our tongue, or never taking a second glance at a provocative body, or never padding an expense account, or never telling a half-truth seems overpowering. Fortunately we serve a forgiving God. But as one of my friends says, "Let's not make Him work overtime."

You and I know we are not faultless, but for starters, we can "act as if" what we do makes a difference. We can act as if we believed in telling the truth and keeping our word. We can act as if we wanted to be faithful to our mate. We can act as if loyalty mattered.

You've no doubt heard about cases where people lived a lie so long they started to believe it. Perhaps this marvel can work in our favor. If we act as if we cared for others long enough, maybe, just maybe, the charade would become the reality. Shakespeare tells us, "All life's a stage." Our job is to bring up the curtain on a new act.

WHAT DOES THE LORD REQUIRE?

Here are some themes your new act might contain. We often think we are living up to the standards only to find out something is missing.

I'm reminded of a story about two youngsters who needed to learn more about the art of sharing. "Darling," scolded the mother, "you shouldn't always keep everything for yourself. I have told you before that you should let your brother play with your toys half of the time."

"I've been doing that, Mom," she replied. "I take the sled going downhill and he takes it going up."

Sometimes in the confusion over what is right and what is wrong, it's good to have a yardstick to measure our performance. Here's one I particularly appreciate: "He has shown you, O man, what is good; And what does the Lord require of you, but to do justly, to love mercy, and to walk humbly with your God?" (Micah 6:8).

The prophet leaves this scripture in the form of a question. Perhaps it's up to us to apply the admonitions and see if they don't bring the outcomes we desire.

Do You Not Teach Yourself?

One thing that has weighed heavily on my mind throughout the preparation of this book is the responsibility of God's servants and pastors. The spate of sorry disclosures about sexual misconduct and financial irresponsibility in the ministry saddens me greatly. Elsewhere I've cited the warning from Christ about how it would be better for someone who offends one of God's little ones to tie a millstone about his neck and jump into the ocean. The Bible is filled with admonitions to those who profess to be "wise" and live otherwise.

This passage from Paul conveys the importance of that responsibility:

> Indeed you are called a Jew, and rest on the law, and make your boast in God, and know His will, and approve the things that are excellent, being instructed out of the law, and are confident that you yourself are a guide to the blind, a light to those who are in darkness, an instructor of the foolish, a teacher of babes, having the form of knowledge and truth in the law. You, therefore, who teach another, do you not teach yourself? You who preach that a man should not steal, do you steal? You who say, "Do not commit adultery," do you commit adultery? You who abhor idols, do you rob temples? You who make your boast in the law, do you dishonor God through breaking the law? For "The name of God is blasphemed among the Gentiles because of you," as it is written (Rom. 2:17–24).

To those ministers who would dare to preach the high words of God and live the low life of heathens I add, "God is not mocked; for whatever a man sows, that he will also reap" (Gal. 6:7). "It is a fearful thing to fall into the hands of the living God" (Heb. 10:31).

David was a man of God who made a number of human mistakes. We looked at his indiscretion with Bathsheba in Chapter 3. He stumbled, but he was always willing to confess his sins and change. His moving words of repentance in Psalm 51 are a powerful tribute to his integrity.

For me, King David represents a clear call to action. There's an interesting reference to David and "integrity" in the New International Version of the Bible. It reads, "I know, my God, that you test the heart and are pleased with integrity—all these things have I given willingly and with honest intent" (1 Chron. 29:17).

Highest honors are bestowed upon David in the New Testament. "I have found David the son of Jesse, a man after mine own heart, which shall fulfill all my will" (Acts 13:22). Later in the same chapter, Paul explains something about David we all would appreciate hearing about ourselves. "For David, after he had served his own generation by the will of God, fell asleep" (Acts 13:36).

What could be a better epitaph for you and me? "He served his own generation by the will of God and fell asleep." Such is the outcome of walking the high road of integrity.

BEN ALEXANDER

You may have wondered about my experience with Ben Alexander aboard flight 712 to Tokyo. If you asked me, "Did this really happen?" I'd have to say, "No, it did not." But if you asked me, "Did I feel the presence of the Lord during my meditations and writing for this book?" I'd have to say, "Yes!" Paul talks about a trip to the third heaven "whether in the body I do not know, or whether out of the body I do not know" (2 Cor. 12:2). For me this was a peak experience with the invisible God of integrity that's more lasting and more meaningful than my encounters with a thousand other visible passengers. And though the event never happened "in the body," the understanding and enlightenment we have shared together in these pages has been unmistakably real.

Before he left to go into action on another "call," Ben asked what I was going to do with this knowledge about integrity and the pain of its loss. I promised I'd write about it . . . in word and deed.

Will you join me in the same? "But those who wait on the Lord shall renew their strength; They shall mount up with wings like eagles, they shall run and not be weary, they shall walk and not faint" (Isa. 40:31).

Notes

Chapter 1

1. *U.S. News & World Report,* 6 April 1987, p. 58.
2. *Unger's Bible Dictionary,* 1966, Moody Press, Chicago, pp. 1128, 29, "Urim."
3. "How to Handle Your Foes: Keep on Shining," *Robert H. Schuller Tells You How to Be an Extraordinary Person in an Ordinary World,* 1985, Fleming H. Revell Company (as reprinted in *Possibilities* Magazine, July/August 1985, p. 23).

Chapter 2

1. "A Nation of Liars?" *U.S. News & World Report,* 23 Feb. 1987, p. 54.
2. "Morality Among the Supply-Siders," *Time,* 25 May 1987, p. 18.
3. Ibid.
4. "How to Raise a Billion Dollars," J. David Schmidt, Christianity Today Institute, 15 May 1987, p. 36.
5. *The Rebirth of America,* Arthur S. DeMoss Foundation, 1986, p. 143.
6. *Business and Professional Pointmakers,* Jacob M. Braude, Prentice-Hall, Inc., Englewood Cliffs, NJ, 1965, p. 112.

Chapter 3

1. "Marriage Just Got Easier," AP, *Pasadena Star News,* 29 June 1987, p. 1.
2. "Trials of an Expert Witness," Elizabeth Loftus, *Newsweek,* 29 June 1987, p. 9.

3. Paraphrase from "Secular Humanism—Not the Only Enemy," Donald G. Bloesch, *Eternity*, Jan. 1982, p. 22.
4. *Los Angeles Times*, 5 July 1987, Part I, p. 24.
5. "Congress Investigates Itself," Peter Osterlund, *Christian Science Monitor*, 7 May 1987, p. 3.
6. *Best Loved Poems* by Hazel Felleman, p. 91: "Myself," by Edgar A. Guest.
7. Horace L. Fenton in the *Latin American Evangelist* (1971).
8. Dennis E. Clark, *The Third World and Missions*, (Waco: Word Books, 1971), 45.

Chapter 5

1. Staff writer, *Time* (29 October 1979): 87.
2. *Heart of Joy: The Transforming Power of Self-Giving*, Servant Publications, 1987 as quoted in *Equipping the Saints*, article on "The Family," by Mother Teresa, May/June 1987, p. 6.
3. Malcolm Muggeridge, *Something Beautiful for God* (New York: Ballantine books, 1971), 58.
4. "Billy Graham: Beacon of Integrity," Dick Capen, *Miami Herald*, 12 April 1987, p. 3C.
5. *Winning through Integrity*, Cliff C. Jones (New York: Ballantine Books, 1985), 58.
6. Katharine L. McEnderfer, "Rosey Grier: A Champion of Love," *Possibilities*, Jan./Feb. 1987, p. 8.
7. "For Town and Team, Honor Is Its Own Reward," William E. Schmidt, *New York Times*, 5/25/87, p. 1.
8. *Miracle at Philadelphia*, Catherine Drinker Bowen (Boston: Little, Brown and Company; 1966), 126.
9. Ibid, p. 127.
10. *Business and Professional Pointmakers*, Jacob M. Braude (Englewood Cliffs, N.J.: Prentice-Hall, Inc., 1965), 73.
11. Ted Engstrom, *The Pursuit of Excellence* (Grand Rapids: Zondervan, 1982).

Chapter 6

1. "How They Have Fallen," Richard S. Sisson, *Moody Monthly*, June 1987, p. 22.
2. Lloyd H. Steffen, *The Christian Century*, "On Honesty and Self-Deception: 'You Are the Man,'" 29 April 1987, p. 403.

Chapter 7

1. *Christian Herald* magazine, July-August 1987, p. 6.
2. James Dobson, Focus on the Family, audio-cassette "Reaching the Unchurched," CS 321, 1986, side two.
3. Ibid., audio cassette.
4. *Christian Herald,* July/August 1987, p. 5.
5. Christianity Today Institute, 15 May 1987, p. 38.
6. Associated Press, 4 August 1987, *Pasadena Star News,* A-8.
7. *Winning through Integrity,* Cliff C. Jones (Ballantine Books, New York, 1985), 84.
8. *Bits and Pieces,* Economics Press, Inc., New Jersey, April 1987, p. 2.
9. "An Interview with Buck Rodgers: Selling Solutions," Gerhard Gschwandtner, Management Review, July 1987, p. 48.
10. Ibid., p. 51.
11. Ibid., p. 48.
12. *Bits and Pieces,* April 1987, p. 12.
13. *Get the Best from Yourself,* Nido Qubein (Englewood Cliffs, NJ: Prentice-Hall, New Jersey, 1983), 60.

Chapter 8

1. *Winning through Integrity,* Cliff C. Jones, p. 56.
2. Bits and Pieces, pp. 20–21.
3. *Halley's Bible Handbook,* Henry H. Halley (Grand Rapids: Zondervan Publishing House, 1959), 158.
4. *The Good Habit of Breaking Bad Habits,* Norman Vincent Peale, Guideposts, Guideposts Associates, Carmel, NY, Feb. 1983, pp. 14–16.

Chapter 9

1. "Perspectives," *Newsweek,* 24 August 1987, p. 11.

Study Guide

Making Integrity Work for You:
A Creative Response

In the following pages we have given you the opportunity to respond to the material presented in the foregoing chapters. Our purpose here is to further challenge and stimulate your thinking in the area of personal integrity. We suggest you use these questions either for personal reflection or as provocative "discussion starters" for small or large groups. Please add questions of your own that may better reflect your particular interests. Obviously there are no right answers. We simply ask you to approach each question openly and without prejudice as you make integrity work for you.

1. Semper Infidelis

1. In this chapter we noted the Marines are still "looking for a few good men" who will be "semper fidelis"—always faithful, always true. Looking beyond the military example and into our individual lives, is it too much to ask that we be "always faithful" to one another? In fact, what does "being faithful" actually mean?
2. What are the main deterrents to "keeping our word"? Are we afraid? Is it low self-esteem? Is it often simply inconvenient to keep our promises? Is it possible to reprogram ourselves to become people of greater integrity? If so, how? What is the process?
3. AIDS is one of the most feared words in the English language today. Is a "do it if it feels good," *value-free sexual activity* going to be forced to bow down before the greater value of integrity? Does a life of integrity mean we will refuse to accept "irresponsible alternative sexual lifestyles?" How do you deal with this issue? How do you talk about it with your friends, your children, your grandchildren?
4. What are your definitions of integrity? What is it *not?* How would you define integrity to a ten-year-old? How do you

feel about Dr. Lewis Smedes' comment that integrity is essentially "promise keeping"?

5. What does the Bible say about integrity? Think back on your favorite stories in Scripture. Who are the people of integrity? What do you respect about their lives and actions? How might those men and women be models for you and your family?

2. One Nation under Greed?

1. In this chapter we suggested the tragedy of Watergate was a watershed event in American ethics. How do you feel about that? Did the events of that scandal set America on any particular collision course with ethics and integrity? If so, are we still on that course? What, if anything, can you do as an individual or group to help prevent such occurrences in the future?

2. Let's talk about money. Inscribed on our currency are the words, "In God we trust." Is this wishful thinking, or do you feel such a phrase is the general consensus of most Americans? Has familiarity with these words possibly created a degree of contempt? What do our spending habits have to do with integrity? What are we teaching our congregations and our children about the relationship between money and ethics?

3. What demands are you prepared to make of organizations that solicit your "donor dollars"? How can you be certain these groups are acting with integrity? Has your "giving pattern" changed in the wake of the recent PTL scandal? If so, why? What will it take for you to start trusting certain nonprofit organizations again?

4. We've suggested that one of the great benefits of recognizing the faults in others is to become more aware of the need to look more carefully at ourselves. What have you learned in this regard? What flaws exist in your own "integrity armor"? What are you prepared to do to change this? How can others help you become more the person you choose to be?

5. If you were to summarize this chapter in a paragraph, what would you say? What was most important to you? What insights, if any, have you "picked up" that you feel can make a difference in your life? When do you intend to put those insights to work for you?

3. When "Wrong" Becomes Right

1. Don Quixote made the statement, "Facts? Facts are the enemies of the truth." I think we'd all agree that humor is often a great cover for what we really believe. Is there any "truth" in Don Quixote's remark? If so, how does that relate to integrity? What is "truth" to you?
2. Some roads "seem right," when, in fact, they may well be broad highways leading to destruction. How are you determining the paths on which you will travel? If you find you're taking shortcuts, how do you tell yourself to get back on the main road?
3. Think technology for a moment. How can these seemingly pleasurable, time-saving—even life-saving—devices possibly be a threat to our value system? Jacques Ellul called this technology the "dominant ideology" in modernized nations. Do you agree? When is it time to say "no" to the proliferation of these "technological marvels"? Has any form of today's technology impacted you in a negative way? If so, how?
4. In this chapter we talked about Lt. Col. Oliver North and his appearance before the committee investigating the use/misuse of funds for the Contras. How are you determining what can only be described as "true North" in your life? What do you value most? Is integrity in living one of your most sought-after virtues? If so, why? If not, why not? If you were Lt. Col. North, would your decisions and actions regarding the Contra issue have been any different? Discuss.
5. A key phrase to understanding our brothers and sisters throughout our ever-shrinking world are the words "cultural sensitivity." How culturally sensitive are you? In your view, is what another culture does "wrong" or simply "different"? How would you describe "cultural integrity"? How do you talk about this global integrity issue with your congregation, your club, friends or children?

4. Our Mandatory Option

1. Is integrity merely optional, or do you feel it should be at the core of your thinking and activity? What would happen if the members of your church, club or family chose for *one week* to live lives of conscious integrity? What would be the results? Would you be willing to engage in such a conscious experiment?

2. How is integrity vital—mandatory—for the intelligent preservation of our society? What about integrity in transportation, political life, sales, parenting, education, marketing, etc? What does this kind of integrity look like? What happens when that integrity becomes simply an option and not a mandate? Are there societies where such a scenario already exists? Would you want to live in such a society? Why? Why not?

3. In this chapter we wrote of several biblical examples of integrity—and lack of it. How do those examples speak to our condition today? Has human nature changed? Are we more insightful than our spiritual forebears in matters of ethics? If so, in what ways?

4. We have encouraged you to *build the kind of integrity you can stake our life on.* What does this phrase mean to you? Is it realistic—even possible—to place integrity on such a high level? Among the many worthy choices in life, *should* integrity necessarily be accorded this preferential status?

5. Look again at the "Christian Survival Compass" on page 61. What other elements could you add to each direction of this moral compass? Do you agree with John Ruskin's comment that "To see clearly is poetry, prophecy and religion all in one"? How does a focus on integrity *improve our vision* of life itself?

5. An Integrity Showcase

1. Who are some of the people you would like to see honored in your "integrity showcase"? Why? What are their qualities? How do they differ from others? Do they possess abilities unavailable to the "common" person? Do you feel you are qualified to be a candidate for such a showcase? If so, why?

2. Mother Teresa is renowned for her patient, unselfish caring for the sick and the dying in Calcutta. Why has her ministry of reaching out to others received such worldwide acclaim? Certainly there are others whose deeds are as noble but who have not received such global notoriety. What makes Mother Teresa different? Does it have anything to do with her personal integrity? If so, in what way?

3. Reread Mother Teresa's poem on page 69 that begins, "When I was homeless." What do these words do to you? How can you incorporate the spirit of her message into your

life and the life of your family? How would you rewrite this poem to reflect your own personal concerns today?

4. Which persons in our "integrity showcase" are most appealing to you? Why? Could any of them be models of integrity to help strengthen your own behavior? Do you feel the qualities of integrity they exhibit are available to you and your family? If you had to give an "integrity" lecture on any one of these in our "showcase," which man or woman would you choose? Why?

5. What kind of moral integrity was demanded of the signers of the U.S. Constitution? How did those early leaders have the foresight to write the document they ultimately produced? Is there a serious danger of the waning of that integrity in our nation today? If so, give examples. Can such a trend toward unethical behavior be reversed? How?

6. Head of Gold, Feet of Clay

1. What does the story of Daniel say to you about integrity? Have you ever had to enter your own "den of lions" because you chose integrity in word or deed? If so, was such integrity worth the risk? Or was it ultimately a risk at all? Explain.

2. How transparently are you willing to live your life? Since integrity is a full-time job, are you prepared to live out that integrity "from head to toe"—in your work, play, with your family, during your times of leisure? What do you think will be some of the obstacles toward living out this kind of integrity?

3. What does "leaning on the Lord" have to do with "standing on your own two feet"? How does Jesus Christ demonstrate His integrity to you? How does that demonstration make you a changed person? Explain.

4. What does it mean to have feet shod with the "preparation of the gospel of peace"? What does integrity have to do with peace? Is there a hidden quality called "integrity" that could reduce the arms race and the threat of nuclear war, while at the same time promote tranquility within our families? What does this kind of integrity "look like"? How do you manifest such integrity in *your* search for peace and contentment?

5. What five things can you do this week to instill an added dimension of integrity to your life? How will you know if your IQ—your integrity quotient—has improved? Are you willing to go about this exercise quietly, without telling

anyone what you are doing? We encourage you to try it. You'll find the results most rewarding.

7. New Rules for a New Millennium

1. Imagine it's midnight, December 31, 1999. In a moment the twenty-first century will be ushered in. What rules in the new millennium—and even braver new world—will be different? Which codes of personal conduct will remain the same? Where will "integrity" stand on your priority list? Where will you *want* it to stand?
2. One of the "rules" we've suggested on page 108 is: "Give of your best in the worst of times." Comment on this statement. If you were consistently able to "give of your best" under these difficult conditions, what would it indicate about your personal integrity? Would such an exercise be worth the effort? Why? Why not?
3. One of the components of integrity is accountability—*not living as a law unto yourself.* What happens when you choose to be accountable to others? Does it make you feel weak? Strong? Confident? How can *choosing to be accountable* protect you from making rash, even bad decisions?
4. What do you think about a 2/4/6 club for yourself and a few of your close friends? List the potential benefits of such a regular get-together. What might you learn about yourself? How could such a group be an "integrity check" for you? Would you be willing to give such a group a try? If so, would you be willing to make a few calls today to find out if others will join you? (You may discover your friends have the same desire for fellowship that demands that high level of accountability.)
5. On page 117, former director of marketing for IBM, "Buck" Rodgers, talks about how IBM was built on three basic beliefs. Take another look at those beliefs carefully and ask yourself: Could those three ideas work for me? If so, keep rereading "Buck" Rodgers' comments, and discover how much of what worked for IBM can work for you. *Starting now!*

8. The High Road to Integrity

1. None of us is perfect. "All have sinned and come short of the glory of God." Integrity has not always been our "middle name." Now, what can you do about it? If you've not been a

person of integrity, how can you restart your integrity engines? Are you willing to believe in a loving, merciful God who is big on forgiveness and short on judgment? Write down a plan of action that reflects the kind of person of integrity you choose to be from this day forward.

2. Take another look at the story of Rahab—a prostitute. While her daily behavior was suspect, her commitment to protect two of the Lord's messengers was a God-send. Is it possible to lead two lives—one committed to and one devoid of integrity? Or do you feel perhaps we don't have the conclusion to Rahab's story? It would have to be speculative, but what do you feel *may have been* the outcome—for Rahab—resulting from her protection of God's servants?

3. Why is the road to integrity such a "high road"? Why is it so tough? What answers do you find to that question in this chapter? What kind of mental and spiritual toughness must you exhibit to be the person of integrity you want to be? What kind of progress would you like to make, say, in the next six months? Write down your integrity goals and share them with a friend.

4. On page 134, we read one of the most beautiful passages in Scripture (Ruth 1:16–17). What thoughts come to your mind as you read these verses? Are you prepared to demonstrate this kind of commitment to another person—to your spouse, children, friends, colleagues? What does this passage say about integrity? What would your world be like if you lived out the message in this passage?

5. Sometimes the greatest obstacles to personal growth are self-imposed bad habits. How can you move more quickly to your "integrity goals" by getting rid of habits that drag you down, sap your energies and destroy your enthusiasm? Are you willing to list those bad habits and then begin a plan to turn them into good, productive behavior? Give three reasons why you should start doing this today.

9. A Call to Action

1. Have you ever had a "Ben Alexander" experience? If so, when? Was it a dream, vision? How did you relate to "Ben" in this chapter? Was he real to you? Who else could he have been? Would you have felt comfortable sitting next to him on that flight to Tokyo? Why? Why not?

2. What do you believe about the "power of one"? Do you believe *you* and your acts of integrity can make a difference? How? When can you expect to see results? List the other "power of one" units in your community. E.g., teachers, pastors, parents, etc. What might happen if these "ones" chose to walk the high road of integrity in all their actions? What kind of a community would you then be living in?

A final word:

We thank you for doing us the courtesy of reading our book. We hope it has challenged, stimulated and provoked you to keep walking that high road of integrity in your personal, family and corporate life. We also urge you to share these pages with a friend, so that your own "power of one" will become the power of two, three and even more.

God bless you.

Sincerely,

Ted W. Engstrom
Robert C. Larson